ISLAM

AN INTRODUCTION

Syed Abul Hasan Ali Nadwi

NADWI
PRESS

Nadwi Press Edition

Find our titles on your favourite online bookstore using the keyword 'Nadwi Press'

Translation of the Qur'ān

It should be perfectly clear that the Qur'ān is only authentic in its original language, Arabic. Since perfect translation of the Qur'ān is impossible, we have used the translation of the meaning of the Qur'ān throughout the book, as the result is only a crude meaning of the Arabic text.

Qur'ānic verses appear in speech marks proceeded by a reference to the Surah and verse number. Sayings (Hadith) of Prophet Muhammad (saw) appear in inverted commas along with reference to the Hadith Book and its Reporter.

CONTENTS

III ISLAMIC SOCIETY: FEATURES, FESTIVALS AND CUSTOMS

Prominent Features:

Important Festivals:

Important Customs:

IV ISLAMIC CULTURE

·VI CONCLUSION

COMPILERS NOTE

The present work is a collection of extracts from Hazrat Maulana Sayyid Abul Hasan Nadwi's published books, articles, and lectures dealing with the theme of the meaning and message of Islam. Due to his acknowledged scholarship, pious lifestyle, and sound understanding of religion, I wished to prepare a book consisting of his writings and discourses that could inform both Muslims and non-Muslims about the authentic nature, principles, and message of Islam. Such a book is a need of the day in view of the growing misunderstanding against Islam so that sincere and objective readers may see for themselves what the simple and pure form of Islam is.

The extracts selected for this book are mainly from Maulana Nadwi's books *The Musalman, Four Pillars of Islam* and his lectures from the platform of "The Message of Humanity". As selections are both from his written works and extempore lectures, a variation in the written and spoken styles naturally exists in the book. No effort has been made to edit the work from this point of view, as the emphasis in it lies on the message, not on the style. I wish to thank all those who helped me in compiling this book, especially Risaluddin Nadwi, and Sulaiman Nadwi who took personal interest in bringing the book to the present form.

May Allah accept this work and guide us all to His pleasure.

Abdullah Hasani Nadwi
Darul Uloom Nadwatul Ulema
Lucknow

PREFACE

Modern Technological advancement has reduced distance and turned the present world into a home whose residents have to live together like family members in spite of differences in their communal, social, national, and religious backgrounds. It is absolutely necessary for co-existence, an accepted norm of the civilized[1] world of today, that mutual relationship among people should be based on cooperation, trust, respect, and goodwill. In order to achieve this end people must make honest and sincere efforts to know, understand, and respect the traits, cultures and beliefs of one another. The state of the affair, however, is different. Although today people from different communities in a country closely share life--shopping, studying, working, and travelling together--they are still very much unfamiliar with the values and beliefs of one another.

In India, for example, Hindus Muslims and followers of several other religions have been living together for centuries and sharing political and social responsibilities, but they remain unfamiliar with the cultural, national, and religious traits of one another in a way which was seen in the past among the people of far-away and distant countries. Their knowledge about one another is superficial and unauthentic. What is more painful is that each community has developed mistrust and hatred for the others' due to political propaganda, wilful distortion of history, and fabricated stories. This is a sad situation and no one community could be held responsible for it.

---

[1]For spelling here and elsewhere in this b ok I have followed A.S. Hornby, Oxford Advanced Learner's *Dictionary* of Current English (London: Oxford University Press, 1974).

It was a common responsibility of leaders of all communities to address to this problem, but presumably not enough effort was made in this direction.

It is, therefore, the first and foremost requirement for peaceful co-existence and for joining hands for noble causes such as serving the motherland and humanity that the followers of different religions must acquire necessary knowledge about one another. If such a relationship is not developed, the energy of all communities, which is a national asset, will be wasted.

In this background there was a need of a book which described Muslims objectively and authentically so that people of other communities could get reliable information about them. For this purpose I earlier wrote a book *The Musalman*, which is available in Urdu and Hindi as well. But as it is difficult for people in the present busy world to read exhaustive books, there remained the need of a book on this subject which would be short but sufficiently informative. I am glad that Sayyid Abdullah Hasani Nadwi (a teacher at Darul Uloom Nadwatul Ulema and son of a famous scholar and writer in Arabic and Urdu, Late Maulana Mohammad Hasani whose Arabic writings won great acclaim from distinguished Arab scholars) took a practical step to address to this need by preparing the present book for an audience comprising sincere people from all communities. The selections are appropriate and reflect the compiler's ability, knowledge and sound judgment. He is a teacher at Darul Uloom Nadwatul Ulema, India, an institution of international fame, and a member of a family which has so sincerely and richly served the cause of learning and culture for a long period of time

In my view this is a useful book containing authentic information which will serve the purpose for which it is prepared.

Sayyid Abul Hasan Ali Nadwi

Guest House
Darul Uloom Nadwatul Ulema
Lucknow

INTRODUCTION

The divine institution of prophethood, according to Islam, began with the descent of the very first man on the earth. Thus the first man Adam, may Allah's blessings be on him, was also the first prophet. After him thousands of prophets were sent for the guidance of humanity who continued to invite people to Allah. They all preached Oneness of Allah, denounced polytheism and infidelity, and tried to persuade people to accept the true faith. They conveyed to them the message of the true faith, taught them about good deeds and informed them about their rewards. They also informed the people about the punishment for holding wrong faith and doing evil deeds.

The progeny of Prophet Adam followed the correct faith for sometime, but later on a number of them went astray and adopted infidelity and polytheism. The prophets of Allah who came later kept on inviting people toward worshipping the One and the Only God, but a number of people rejected their teachings and even opposed them by all means available.

When Prophet Muhammad, blessings and peace be on him, called the people of his time to Islam, some accepted his message while others rejected and opposed. The opponents fought Islam tooth and nail in Makkah and did everything within their capacity to persecute the Prophet, blessings and peace be on him, and the first adherents to Islam. They dragged Muslims, like Bilal and Khabbab, in the streets of Makkah, humiliated and beat mercilessly even honourable people like Abu Darr Ghifari and Abu Bakr, and killed some, like the parents of Ammar Bin Yasir, may Allah be pleased with all these suffering souls. Such a hostile situation made it so difficult for Muslims to live in Makkah that a number of them, including the Prophet's daughter and his son-in-law Uthman Bin Affan, had to migrate in helplessness to Abyssinia. In spite of such severe persecution, no Muslim ever relinquished Islam and returned to infidelity. When the Roman emperor of that time, Harqul, learnt about it from Abu Sufyan, he correctly commented:

Faith works like
this when its
felicity pierces
the hearts.

The sincere adherence of the Prophet's companions to Islam and their readiness to undergo any consequent suffering ultimately touched the hearts of people and they slowly started coming to the fold of Islam in spite of all opposition. The Prophet, blessings and peace be on him, and his Companions continued incessantly to invite people to Islam. Whoever accepted Islam did so on its merits and immediately became a preacher of the faith. The Prophet, blessings and peace be on him, himself took the opportunity to invite members of two tribes from Madinah, Aws and Khazraj, when they came to Makkah to perform Hajj. They accepted Islam and all the other members of these two tribes came to the fold of Islam later when the Prophet of Allah, blessings and peace be on him, emigrated to Madinah. After the conquest of Makkah, the residents thereof embraced Islam. Then the delegations of the Arab tribes from all over the country came to Madinah and professed faith in Islam. When they returned, they propagated the message of Islam in their areas. Soon the whole Arabia came to the fold of Islam. As soon as it happened, the Prophet, whose mission was to convey the message of Islam throughout the world, wrote letters and sent delegations to the rulers of the neighbouring countries.

In fact, Islam spread all over the world through preaching and won adherents on the strength of its eternal truth and beauty. The Muslim rulers did not exercise their power to spread Islam. It were the pious Muslims outside the royal courts who took the message of Islam to the doors of the people and knocked at their hearts. It is well known that about ninety-hundred thousand people accepted Islam in India on the hands of Hazrat Moinuddin Chishti, a Sufi saint. History has preserved the name of a trader Sulaiman whose virtuous dealings and preachings won the hearts of people living in the islands of northern Asia and engendered in them a desire to accept Islam.

History also records another similar event in which one single Muslim served as a cause for the people of a place to accept Islam. A Muslim trader once arrived an island of northern India and stayed for a night at the house of an old lady. Finding that she was greatly distressed, he inquired into the reason. She explained to him that the people of that island offered a young girl to the rising sea every year at a particular night to appease it. The girl chosen for that purpose was adorned with elegant dress and ornaments and made to sit on the bank of the sea at night where the waves devoured her sometime before the sunrise. As it was her daughter's turn that night, she was sad for her. The trader took the old lady into confidence and requested her to dress him up as a woman and hand him over to the people who would come to collect her daughter at night. The old lady did as instructed.

At night the sea rose and its ferocious waves moved roaring toward the Muslim traveller who was made to sit on the bank of the sea. The man, however, remained patient entrusting himself to the care of Allah and kept himself engaged in His remembrance. Soon the water receded without causing any harm to him. In the morning the people of the island came to the seaside and were truly surprised to find a man sitting there instead of a girl. The Muslim trader informed them about the whole incident, introduced Islam to them and explained that the only author of benefit or harm was Allah in Whom people should repose their trust and Whom they should worship. As a result the residents of the island accepted Islam. Numerous such instances are authentically recorded in history in which sincere efforts of an individual or a small group of people brought the residents of an area to the fold of Islam. Wherever Islam spread, it has been by virtue of its intrinsic merits and appeal.

The antogonists of Islam propagate that Islam was spread by sword. This is a gross misrepresentation of Islam and its teachings. Muslims have nowhere forced any individual, group of people, or an entire population to accept Islam under a threat to their lives. In fact, Muslims cannot do so because forcing anybody to accept Islam is categorically forbidden in Islam. The Quran clearly states this principle in the following words:

Let there be no
compulsion in religion:
Truth stands out clear
from error.
    [II: 256]

By nature, Islam is not at all ready to open its doors to people who profess faith in it by tongue and remain unbelievers at heart. Islam categorizes such people as hypocrites (*Munafiqeen*) and does not, in fact, accept them as true believers. It is a historical fact that Muslims once ruled over approximately half of the population of the entire world. Had the Muslim rulers wished to force their non-Muslim subjects to accept Islam, none under their rule would have remained a non-Muslim. The large number of non-Muslims living now in countries which were once ruled by Muslims testifies to the fact that non-Muslims were never forced to relinquish their faith in favour of Islam in the days when Muslim rulers were in a position to impose their will on them.

Commenting on the above accusation against Islam, Maulana Qasim Nanotwi, a great Indian scholar, raises a question for the sincere people to ponder: How those Muslims who are said to have used sword to spread Islam themselves accepted Islam? Who used sword against them to force them to accept Islam? The residents of Madinah al-Munawwara accepted Islam without any expedition against them. The people of Makkah al-Mukarrama accepted Islam without force. The people of Yemen entered the fold of Islam by their free will. No army was sent to Iraq to force its people to accept Islam. The Christian religious leaders of Baitul Maqdis handed over the key of the city to the Muslim Caliph Umar ibn Khattab without any war. No sword was raised against those ninety-hundred thousand people in India who entered the fold of Islam at the hands of Hazrat Moinuddin Chishti.

The objective of the Muslim expeditions was never to capture new lands and establish on the face of the earth a huge

Muslim empire. Its true and only objective was to extend the message of Oneness of Allah to mankind far and wide, safeguard the weak in the society from being put to bondage and servitude by the rich and the tyrant, and introduce all to the natural freedom ensured by faith in the true supremacy of the One God over all. Hafiz ibn Katheer writes in his famous book *Al-Bidaya Wan-Nihaya*, Vol. VII, (Page 38), that when the Muslim army entered the Persian empire and stood face to face with the Persian army, the commander of the Persian army Rustam wished to speak to a representative of the Muslims. The Muslim commander S'ad bin Waqqas sent Mughira bin Sho'ba to him. Rustam told Mughira that the Muslims were the neighbours of the Persian people and that the Persian people had always abstained from inflicting any harm upon them. Thus, he added, the Muslims should return to their cities and could come to Persia for trade which would not be denied to them by the Persian government. Mughira replied to Rustam that the aim of the Muslim army was not to achieve material gain but to attain true success in the hereafter. God the Almighty, he added, had sent a Prophet to them who had been appointed by God to convey the message of the True Faith to mankind and challenge those who opposed it. God had also promised that those who accepted that religion would prevail and those who opposed it would meet disgrace.

Rustam asked Mughira: What is that religion that your Prophet has brought to you?

Mughira replied: The most important teaching of that religion is affirming that there is no one worthy of worship except Allah, that Muhammad, blessings and peace be on him, is the Prophet of Allah, and that whatever he conveys from Allah is true.

Rustam said: This is a good teaching. What comes after it?

Mughira replied: To emancipate man from bondage to man (i.,e. to relieve the weak from the yoke of the powerful and grant all human beings equal status in the essential human sense), and lead mankind to take the One and the Only God, Allah, as their Master, and to worship Him alone.

Rustam said: This is also a good teaching of your religion. If we accept your religion, will you return to your cities (without waging a war against us and capturing our lands)?

Mughira replied: By God, we will do so. Then we will not come even close to your cities, except, maybe, for trade or any other need of this kind.

Rustam was greatly surprised. When Mughira returned to his army, Rustam tried to encourage the leaders of his nation to accept Islam but failed.

Also, Islamic expeditions were not taken to accumulate wealth but to promote man's free and dignified relationship with God under the guidance of the true teachings of Islam. Imam Abu Yusuf, one of the most reputed Muslim jurists, has recorded in his famous book *Kitabul Khiraj* that Abdul Hammed ibn Abdur Rahman wrote the Muslim Caliph of the time Umar bin Abdul Azeez that the non-Muslim residents of Hira, the Jews, the Christians, and the Majoosis who owed large sums of money as *Jizya*[1] to the Islamic state, Abdul Hameed asked the Caliph Umar bin Abdul Azeez for permission to collect *Jizya* from the new converts even after their acceptance of Islam so as to avoid financial loss to the state. Umar bin Abdul Azeez, may Allah be pleased with him, wrote back that Allah, the Magnificent, had sent Prophet Muhammad, blessings and peace be on him, to convey the message of Islam, not to collect wealth and so those non-Muslims who accepted Islam would not be asked to pay any money for *Jizya*. They would rather pay *Zakah* (poor-due) in accordance with the Islamic laws as all Muslims do.

This is the real spirit of Islam. If any Muslim ruler has ever violated Islamic laws, Islam cannot be held responsible for it.

Islam has been misrepresented by its detractors for long. It is high time now that it should be studied objectively and judged on its own grounds. With this purpose in mind the present book, introducing Islam as completely and objectively as possible, is offered to the interested readers.

A.A.N

[1] *Jizya* is a tax paid by non-Muslims for all state services that are provided to them by an Islamic government. Muslims pay *Zakah* in cash or kind to the Islamic state on annual basis and are also asked to contribute for emergencies and defend their country in times of war--obligations from which non-Muslim residents are exempted.

**In the name of Allah, the Most Beneficent,
the Most Compassionate**

I

ISLAM

Meaning, Nature and Scope

Islam means surrendering oneself totally and unconditionally to Allah. In Islam the rules of religion are applicable to life in total. This fact cannot be fully appreciated unless one duly comprehends the relationship of man with God as enunciated in Islam. According to the teachings of Islam, every Muslim is a faithful bondsman of Allah. His relationship with Allah is permanent and comprehensive. It is deep as well as wide, personal as well as general. It is related in the Quran:

*O ye who believe! enter
into Islam wholeheartedly;
and follow not the footsteps
of the Evil One, for he is
to you an avowed enemy.*
[II: 208]

In Islam there is no division of loyalty, or reservation of any kind. It does not entertain any division such as "this is mine and that is thine"; or "one share for the state, the other for God, and the third for the family and tribe"; or "one part for religion and one for politics". In Islam all belongs to Allah. In it all endeavours of a Muslim are essentially worship. A Muslim stands in front of his Lord as a bondsman totally dependent on His mercy. The teachings of Islam cover life in totality. Nobody is allowed to introduce any change in them. Even the greatest scholar or Islamic leader of a time has no right to introduce a change in an Islamic injunction if it is explicitly laid down in the Quran as final.

Allah requires from believers that they practise Islam fully. not partially as they do now-a-days. Unfortunately, Muslims in general have now moved quite far away from the teachings of Islam in, for example, codes of culture, customs of marriage. and traditions of inheritance. There are Muslims whose understanding of the tenets of the Islamic faith is clear and correct, but they are negligent toward practising even obligatory deeds of worship. There are, on the other hand. others who observe Islamic injunctions both in matters of faith and worship, but they remain highly untrustworthy in morals and dealings. They do not miss an opportunity to deceive: they dishonestly measure and weigh their goods less while selling. cheat their business partners, and cause trouble to their neighbours. The true teachings of Islam are, nevertheless. clearly related in the following traditions of the Prophet. blessings and peace be on him:

"A Muslim is he from whose hands and
tongue other Muslims are safe. "
and
"None of you is a true believer unless his
neighbour is safe from his mischief. "

2

Unfortunately, there are some Muslims who have wrongly excluded dealings and morals from religion. They think that Islam as a religion comprises only the tenets of belief and rituals of worship. They, thus, remain heedless, for example, to the value of honesty in dealings. Fulfillment of a promise, carefulness in dealing with a trust, and honesty in giving due share to the rightful, which are essential teachings of Islam, have no meaning for them. They feel free in disregarding others' just claims on them, do not observe religious rules in dealings, and do whatever suits their mundane interest.

The Companions of the Prophet of Allah who were groomed under the special disciplinary care of the Prophet, blessings and peace be on him, observed the teachings of Islam in total and emerged as true living models of Islam. Their lives--belief, worship, dealings, morals, celebrations, earnings, and ways of governing a state--fully corresponded to the injunctions of the Islamic Shari'a[1]

Value of Faith in Islam

The value of man's bondsmanship to his Lord is based on the correctness of his faith. If a person's faith is incorrect, his deeds, even his worship, are not acceptable to Allah. But if his faith is correct, even a small number of good deeds may suffice for his eternal salvation. Thus, the most important obligation of a Muslim is to learn about things in which he has to believe and which he has to practise. These tenets of faith are fundamental in order for a person to qualify as a Muslim. They

---

[1]Following the examples of Prophet Muhammad and his Companions, all Muslims must carefully observe the teachings of Islam in total. A detailed discussion of this theme is presented in Chapter V of this book.

are commonly shared by Muslims throughout the world and are as follows:

Oneness of Allah (*Tawheed*)

Belief in Oneness of Allah is the first and foremost tenet of the Islamic faith. It does not leave any space for an intermediary between the worshipper and his Lord in matters of worship and supplication. It also does not allow any room for belief in the diversity of gods, or in the existence of a person as God's reflection, or in God merging with any of His creatures to become one with him. Instead, in Islam a believer clearly confesses that there is no god but Allah, the Almighty, the Independent. He has no father, no son, and no associate of any kind. He alone is the Creator of the universe, exercises complete administration of the world, and holds full control of the land and the sky. He does not need help from anybody.

Allah has always existed and shall exist for ever. His attributes are perfect, worthy of praise and glory. He is above all limitations and weaknesses, whatsoever. His knowledge encompasses all and everything. This whole universe came into existence at His will. He is the Living, the Hearing, the Seeing. There is none like Him. He alone deserves worship, the highest manifestation of reverence. It is He Who cures the sick, provides sustenance to creatures, and removes hardship from the suffering. To take anything except Allah as deity, to bow or prostrate in front of it in devotion, and to supplicate to it for favours which are only in Allah's power (for example, granting a baby, bringing luck, reaching a devotee for help

4

anywhere, hearing everything from any distance, and knowing the secrets of heart) is called, in Islamic terminology, *Shirk* (polytheism). It is the most serious sin which is not forgiven unless the person committing it offers sincere repentance.

It is related in the Quran that Allah's power is such that when He intends to do a thing, He simply says "Be", and it becomes (*Yassen*: 82). He does not dwell in any specific place or direction. Whatever He wills comes to pass, for nothing can ever happen against His will. He is absolutely independent. Nobody can order Him for anything or question Him about any of his actions. Wisdom is His attribute and all His actions reflect wisdom, ultimately leading to good. None except Him is the true Lord.

Fate, good or bad, has been decreed by Allah. He knows in advance things that are to happen in the future and causes them to come to pass.

He has created the Angels, who are high in rank and close to Him in relationship. The Devils (*Shayateen*) are also His creatures who are a source of evil for mankind. He has also created the Jinns.

The Quran is a book revealed by Allah. Its words as well as their intended meaning are all from Allah. It is complete and safe from interpolation and change. A person who believes that an addition or deletion had taken place in it is not a Muslim.

It is true that the dead will be brought to life again on an appointed day. Accountability, reward, and punishment are true. The Heaven and the Hell exist in reality.

It is true that Allah sent prophets to mankind in the world. It is also true that Allah sent His commandments to inform and educate His bondsmen through the prophets. Muhammad, blessings and peace be on him, is the last of Allah's prophets. No prophet will be sent after him. The message brought by him is for the whole world. In this exceptional privilege and on some other points of preference, he excels all other prophets. The faith of a person in Islam is not valid and complete unless he affirms faith in the prophethood of Muhammad, blessings and peace be upon him. No other religion is acceptable to Allah and can ensure salvation in the hereafter. Nobody is exempted on account of his piety and godliness from following the injunctions of the Islamic Shari'a.

Abu Bakr Siddique was the rightly chosen *Imam* and *Khalifa*, vicegerent, after Prophet Muhammad, blessings and peace be upon him. After Abu Bakr, Umar ibn Khattahb Uthman bin Affan, and Ali bin Abi Talib were all rightly chosen to this office. The Companions of the Prophet are the leaders of the Muslims in religion. It is forbidden to mention them in a derogatory way. It is obligatory on Muslims to hold them in esteem and respect.

II

PILLARS OF ISLAM

After faith (*Iman*) the most important pillar of Islam is worship (*'Ibadah*) which is the main objective behind man's creation. Allah has stated in the Quran:

And I raised man
and jinn so that
they worship Me.
    [L1: 56]

According to the Islamic Shari'a, four religious services are obligatory on every adult Muslim, man and woman, which are called the four pillars of Islam:

(1) *Salah*, i.e. Prayers offered five times daily, (2) *Zakah*, i.e. Poor-due given on wealth once a year, (3) *Sawm*, i.e. Fasting in the month of Ramadan annually, and (4) *Hajj*, i.e. Pilgrimage to Makkah performed once in lifetime provided one has sufficient means to undertake the journey.[1] If one denies the obligatoriness of any of these pillars, he ceases to be a Muslim.

---

[1] I have used the Arabic terms *Salah, Zakah,* and *Hajj* in the text instead of their English counterparts *Prayer, Poor-due,* and *Pilgrimage* for the sake of their specificity to refer to Islamic rituals. For the fourth pillar of Islam, *Sawm,* however, I have used the English term *Fasting* simply because in some Muslim countries people are more familiar with its Persian and Urdu counterpart *Roza* for liunguistic reasons. Wherever necessary I have also given the English term to facilitate the reader.

If a person forsakes them permanently, he too is considered as one dissociating himself from the group of Muslims.

SALAH (Prayer): First Pillar

Of all forms of worship in Islam, *Salah*, prayers offered five times a day, is of foremost importance. It is a fundamental pillar of Islam and a practice distinguishing Muslims from followers of other religions. In view of its importance it is considered as a line of demarcation between Islam and all other unIslamic ways of life. Allah commands the believers:

And establish
worship and be
not of those who
ascribe partners
(Unto Him).
[XXX:31]

The Prophet of Allah, blessings and peace be upon him, also emphasizes the importance of *Salah* in the following words:

Renouncing Salah
(Prayer) is (a line
of demarcation) between
(Allah's) slave and
infidelity.

In another Tradition the same theme has been underscored in these words:

8

The line of demarcation
between Faith and
infidelity is renouncement
of *Salah* (Prayer).

Salah safeguards faith and leads to ultimate salvation. Allah has mentioned it as a basic condition for His guidance and a sign of piety on the part of a Muslim. It is obligatory on all Muslims, free or slave, healthy or sick, resident or traveller, and has to be offered in all conditions. If a Muslim is unable to stand up, he should offer his prayers sitting. If unable to sit, he is allowed to pray in a reclining or prostrating posture. If even this is not possible for him, he can pray by gestures. But he must pray. Muslims are required to pray even in the battlefield (which is done in a specific way and is known as Prayer of Fear (*Salatul Khawf*). They also pray while undertaking a journey, although for their convenience in the journey all four-Rak'ah obligatory *Salah* are reduced to two-Rak'ah *Salah*. *Salah* is so important and fundamental that even a Prophet is not exempted from it. It is to the believer what water is to the fish. It accords shelter and peace to the believer. If offered with due sincerity, it never lets a believer stoop down to the worship of a false god, accept a lifestyle of ignorance, or adopt any immoral behaviour. Allah states in the Quran:

For Prayer restrains
from shameful and
unjust deeds.
    [XXIX : 45]

9

Salah Sustenance for the Soul

As man was destined to be the vicegerent of God on earth, indeed a very delicate and special position, Allah put in him desires and needs as well as emotions and feelings. He feels the burning of love, pangs of sorrow, and sweetness of joy. He looks around with an innate curiosity to learn about things and possesses a great ability to explore the hidden treasures of the earth to his advantage. In view of his delicate responsibility as vicegerent of God on earth, man was not required to perform the forms of worship such as continuously standing in prayers, or bowing in *Ruku'* (kneeling position), or lying in prostration, or glorifying God as the planets in the sky, or mountains, or other living beings and non-living things on the earth were required to do. A special form of worship was then needed for man which would match with his nature and responsibility as God's vicegerent in the scheme of creation.

Prayer was necessary for man because through it he could satisfy an innate urge in his nature, fulfill the objective of his creation, appease the voice of his conscience, express his gratitude to his Lord, and receive sustenance for his heart and soul. It was also necessary, on the other hand, that the form of worship prescribed for him should fully match with his human needs as well as his needs as vicegerent of God. The form of worship prescribed for him should be like a dress which would fit him well and look appropriate, neither loose nor tight, nor long nor short.

Salah, the Islamic form of worship, is, in fact, like a befitting dress for man perfectly suiting his nature as well as his responsibility in the universe. It does not need any addition or deletion, whatsoever. Allah clearly states in the Quran:

Verily, all things
have We created in
proportion and measure.
    [LIV : 49]

Salah is offered five times a day and has to be said at specified times as ordained by Allah. The number of *Rak'ahs* performed in *Salah* is also fixed and has to be observed without any alteration.

How *Salah* Is Offered

Salah is offered in such an atmosphere of reverence and devotion, awe and carefulness, propriety and seriousness, hope and aspiration, and mutual cooperation and togetherness which is not discerned in the form of worship prescribed in any other religion. We can appreciate *Salah* by trying to understand the wisdom behind the rules and instructions that are to be observed in offering it. With this in mind we will take a look at the etiquette and form of *Salah*, recitations done in it, and ways to begin and end it.

Prayer Call (*Adhan*)

Let us take first the prayer call, *Adhan*, which is raised five times a day from the minaret of a mosque to call Muslims to join the congregational prayers. It is quite familiar everywhere as there would hardly be a city, town, village, or community, even in an area of mixed population, which does not echo with this call. The words of the prayer call are as follows:

Allah is the greatest
Allah is the greatest;
Allah is the greatest
Allah is the greatest.

I bear witness that
there is no god but Allah;

I bear witness that there
is no god but Allah.

I bear witness that
Muhammad is the Prophet
of Allah;

I bear witness that Muhammad
is the Prophet of Allah.

Come to prayers;
Come to prayers.

Come to prosperity;
Come to prosperity.

Allah is the greatest;
Allah is the greatest.
There is no god but Allah.

The call which is thus given for *Salah* announces not only the objective and value of *Salah*; it also proclaims the objective of Islam and value of *Tawheed* (Oneness of Allah) with clarity, completeness, brevity and beauty. In this way *Adhan* enunciates the tenets of the Islamic faith clearly and effectively. This is the only religious call of its kind which is free from accompaniment of any musical instrument and external adornment and which contains so fully the gist of the message of its religion.

Adhan is a proclamation of the magnificence and grandeur of Allah asserting in clear and unwavering words that He is surely the greatest. There is also an attestation in it to the Oneness of Allah and to the prophethood of Muhammad, blessings and peace be upon him. Then it is an invitation to prayers announcing that prayers ensure success in this world and in the hereafter, as success in the true sense of the term can be achieved neither here nor in the hereafter by any other means. With these proclamations *Adhan* manifests a nobility which appeals to the heart and mind simultaneously and draws the attention of the Muslims as well as non-Muslims. This call makes the lazy agile and the forgetful mindful by declaring that the time has come for them to offer prayers to their Lord.

Ablution (*Wudu*)

Muslims are required to attain cleanliness and perform *Wudu* (ablution) for *Salah* (prayer). It is related in the Quran:

O ye who believe!
when ye prepare
for prayer, wash
your faces, and
your hands (and arms)
to the elbows;
rub your heads (with water);
and (wash) your feet
to the ankles.
If ye are in a state
of ceremonial impurity,
bathe your whole body.
But if ye are ill,
or on a journey,
or one of you cometh
from offices of nature,
or ye have been
in contact with women,
and ye find no water,
then take for yourselves
clean sand or earth,
and rub therewith
your faces and hands.
God does not wish
to place you in difficulty,
but to make you clean,
and complete
His favour to you,
that ye may be grateful.
    [V : 7]

14

If a Muslim attains cleanliness and makes *Wudu* (ablution) duly with faith and consciousness of accountability,[2] he finds in himself readiness, alertness, mindfulness, and reverence with which to proceed to prayers. He is thus so very well prepared to begin his *Salah* and acquire its innate effulgence and tranquillity.

The Prophet of Allah, blessings and peace be upon him, has also instructed Muslims to brush their teeth with *Miswak* (soft twig brush) as a part of ablution as this act would help a Muslim in fully benefitting from the virtues of *Wudu* (ablution) and prepare him for *Salah* (which is, in spirit, a believer's conversation with his Lord duly accompanied with supplication). The Prophet, blessings and peace be upon him, has laid so much emphasis on this practice that he once said, "If I did not fear that my followers might find it hard to follow, I would have ordered them to brush their teeth with *Miswak* at he time of all (obligatory) prayers" (Bukhari and Muslim).

Wudu has to be performed before *Salah* (prayer). *Wudu* is a term referring to a specific method of attaining cleanliness without which one is not allowed to perform *Salah*. In *Wudu*,

---

This means that the Muslim concerned should have full trust in the promises of Allah and in the rewards of good deeds as reported by the Prophet of Allah, blessings and peace be upon him, and perform virtuous deeds with eagerness and reverence. Such a state of heart and mind plays a great role is securing Allah's approval. It is reported by Abu Huraira that the Prophet of Allah, blessings and peace be upon him, said, "When a believer makes *Wudu* (ablution) and washes his face, all the sins committed by him with his eyes are washed away with water or with the last drop of water, as a result of which he is fully cleansed of his sins." It is further related by Muslim and Muatta, "When he washes his feet, all the sins committed by him with his feet are washed away." (*Tumidhi*) first the hands are washed up to the wrist three times. Then the mouth is cleaned with water thrice. After that the inner part of the nose is washed three times. Then one washes his face thrice from the top of the forehead to the lowest part of the chin, and from the tip of one ear to that of the other. Thereafter the right hand is washed up to the elbow three times; the left hand is then washed in the same way. Then both the hands. wet with water, are moved once over the hair of the head. Then the feet are washed up to the ankles thrice, first the right foot, then the left. [3] Attending to natural calls, passing air, or falling asleep makes the *Wudu* void. Unless *Wudu* is void, one can perform prayers of several times with it.

Deeds Done in the Mosque

After performing *Wudu* (ablution) a Muslim enters a mosque. First, he individually says his prayers, *Sunnah* or *Nafl* [4] If he has done them at home, he sits quietly and waits for the congregational prayer to begin. He may then engage himself in the recitation of the Quran or in any other form of remembrance of Allah. As the time of the congregational prayer arrives, a call (*Iqamah*) [5] is given which consists of

---

[3] Washing the said parts of the body three times is a *Sunnah* (a practice established by the Prophet, blessings and peace be on him). *Wudu*, however, is valid if these parts are washed twice or even once.
[4] Extra *Salah* following the tradition of the Prophet of Islam, blessings and peace be upon him, to earn more rewards.
[5] *Iqamah* is a call given to announce the commencement of a regular congregational prayer.

16

words said in *Adhan* (prayer call) with the addition of two sentences:

Salah is going to begin,
Salah is going to begin.

Congregational Prayer

All Muslims present in the mosque leave their individual engagements to join the congregational prayer (*Salatul Jama'ah*) and stand side by side in rows. A *Hafiz* (one who has committed the whole Quran to memory), an Islamic scholar or any other learned Muslim leads the prayer[2]. Pronouncing the words *Allaho Akbar* ("Allah is greatest"), he raises his hands up to the tip of his ears and then folds them respectfully around his waist in the front. He stands in front of the believers and thus begins the prayer. Then the Imam (leader) as well as the followers recite at heart the following supplication:

O Allah! You are the
author of excellence,
Your name is auspicious,
Your position is exalted,

---

[2]In Islam the Imams of mosques (who lead prayers) or religious scholars do not form any specific class of priests and are not indispensable for conducting prayer services. Any qualified Muslim can discharge this religious function. Now-a-days, however, the Imams and Muadh-dhins are appointed to perform the designated services in most mosques for administrative purposes and are paid by the Muslims of the localities or from the income of the *Awqaf.*

17

*and there is none worthy
of worship except You.*

Then, if the *Salah* (prayer) is the one in which recitation has to be made loudly, the Imam starts the recitation of a*l-Fatiha*, a chapter from the Quran which is recited in every *Rak'ah* of *Salah*. This chapter marks the opening of the Quran and contains, in brief, the gist of Islamic teachings. It is the most commonly read chapter of the Quran and holds a position of great eminence in Islam. Its text is presented below with translation.

*In the name of God,
Most Gracious, Most
Merciful.*

*Praise be to God,
the Cherisher and
Sustainer of the Worlds;*

*Most Gracious, Most
Merciful;
Master of the Day
of Judgment.*

*Thee do we worship,
and Thine aid we seek.*

Show us the straight way,

the way of those on whom
thou hast bestowed Thy grace,
those whose (portion)
is not wrath,
and who go not astray.
   [1 : 1-7]

At the end of the recitation of this chapter, the leader as well as the followers say *Ameen*, which means, "O Allah! accept our prayers."

After *al-Fatiha*, the Imam recites such verses of the Quran which easily come to his mind. The meaning and message of these verses have a further appeal to the hearts and minds of the worshippers, thus transforming *Salah* (prayers), which is essent ally a form of worship, into an effective medium of instruction. Two short chapters of the Quran which are commonly recited in *Salah* are written down here with translation:

(1)   *In the name of God,*
      Most Gracious, Most
      Merciful.

      By (the token of)
      Time (through the
      Ages),

      verily Man
      is in loss,

except such as have Faith,
and do righteous deeds,
and (join together)
in the mutual teaching
of Truth, and of
Patience and Constancy.
　　[CIII : 1-3]

(2)　*In the name of God,*
　　Most Gracious,
　　Most Merciful.

　　Say: He is God,
　　the One and Only;
　　God, the Eternal, Absolute;

　　He begetteth not,
　　nor is He begotten;
　　and there is none
　　Like unto Him.
　　　　[CXII : 1-4]

After reciting verses of the Quran the Imam (leader) says *Allaho Akbar* ("Allah is greatest") with which he and the followers bow down in the kneeling position called *Ruku'*. In this position they recite thrice or more *Subhana rabbiyal azeem* ("Glory to my Sustainer Who is great"). Then the Imam says, *Same Allaho Iiman hamidah* ("Allah heard him who glorified Him"). With these words the Imam and the followers stand erect for a while in which position the followers say *Rabbana lakal hamd* ("Lord! for You is all praise"). Then the Imam goes in prostration saying *Allaho akbar* ("Allah is greatest") and the followers follow him. In prostration the forehead and nose of the believers touch the ground, palms of their hands recline against the ground, elbows are erected above separated from their sides, and knees are placed on the ground. In prostration they recite *Subhana rabbiyal 'ala* ("Glory to my Sustainer Who is sublime") thrice or more. After that they rise saying *Allaho akbar* ("Allah is greatest") and sit down on their feet folded respectfully. They offer a second prostration immediately after the first one in the same way. In prayers prostration (*Sujood*) is the act in which a worshipper comes closest to Allah and achieves His highest pleasure and appreciation. It is narrated in an Authentic Tradition:

A bondsman is
closest to his Lord
in the state of prostration.
So supplicate abundantly
in that position.

Therefore, a worshipper considers this opportunity very precious and opens his heart to his Lord in prostration.

The believers offering *Salah* then stand up for the second *Rak'ah* (unit) and complete it and the other following *Rak'ahs* in the same way. After each two *Rak'ahs* the worshippers take a sitting position which is called *Q'ada*. If the *Salah* is of more than two *Rak'ahs* and the worshippers have to stand up for the third *Rak'ah*, they say only the following words in that position:

All reverence, prayer,
and sanctity are for
Allah. Peace be on
you, O Prophet, and
the mercy of Allah
and His blessings.
Peace be on us and
on the virtuous bondsmen
of Allah. I bear
witness that there
is no god except
Allah, and I bear
witness that Muhammad
is his slave and
messenger.

In a two-*Rak'ah Salah*, which is to end after *Q'ada* with two salutations, the following supplications are added after the words mentioned above.

O Allah! bestow Your
blessings on Muhammad
and his progeny as
You bestowed blessings
on Ibrahim and
his progeny; verily
You are the Praiseworthy,
the Majestic. O Allah!
bestow abundance on
Muhammad and his
progeny as You bestowed

abundance on Ibrahim
and his progeny; verily
You are the Praiseworthy,
the Majestic.

Our Lord! Give us
good in this world
and good in the hereafter;
and defend us from the
torment of the Fire.
        [II : 201]

O Allah! I seek
refuge in You
from the punishment
of hell and
the punishment of
grave. Lord,
I seek refuge
in You from the
trials of life and
death and from
the harm of the mischief
of the Maseeh
al-Dajjal (Anti-Christ).

Prayer Contributing to Worshippers' Self-Confidence

After a worshipper glorifies Allah and invokes blessings and peace on Prophet Muhammad in *Salah*, he too gets a share in the blessings and peace thus invoked, of which he is truly in need and which he so eagerly wishes to achieve. When he says in his recitation, *Assalamo alaina wa 'ala 'ibadil lahis saliheen* ("Peace be on us and on the virtuous bondsmen of Allah"), he knows that he is, beyond the limitations of time and clime, also included in the supplication for the virtuous people and shares with them Islamic peace, brotherhood, and mercy. This creates in him a self-confidence which dispels from his heart feelings of frustration and outdatedness and helps him look at himself as one belonging to a large group of worshippers including as distinguished people as the learned, the virtuous, and the pious.

They are the party
of God. Truly it is
the party of God that
will achieve felicity.
[LVIII : 22]

After that the worshipper prays for himself and seeks refuge in Allah against punishment of hell, punishment of grave, trials of life and death, and mischief of the Dajjal (Anti-Christ) as these are such things from which Allah's protection must be sought. The Prophet of Allah, blessings and peace be on him, has said in a Hadith: "No Messenger has come to the world after Prophet Noah who did not warn his people against the Dajjal (Anti-Christ). I, too, warn you against him and instruct you to be careful about him."

Completion of Prayer

At the end of *Salah* in which the worshipper tries to observe all etiquette as best as possible, he admits his limitation for not being able to worship his Lord as He deserved to be worshipped and ends his *Salah* with the following words taught for this purpose to Abu Bakr by the Prophet, blessings and peace be on him:

O Allah! I have
done great harm
to myself. There
is none else
except You who
could forgive
my sins. Forgive
me by Your special
mercy and kindness
and have pity on
me. Verily, You are
the Forgiving, the
Merciful.

Thus *Salah* is concluded with a realization of shortcomings on the part of the worshipper which is a most befitting ending of a virtuous deed.

Importance of Mosque

Constructed with the objective of worshipping Allah, mosques reflect simplicity and seriousness, tranquillity and refinement, and spirituality and peacefulness and symbolize the principle of *Tawheed* (Oneness of Allah). In these qualities mosques stand distinguished from places of worship established by other religions.

(Lit it such a Light)
in houses, which God
hath permitted to be
raised to honour; for the
celebration, in them, of
His name; in them is
He glorified in the
mornings and the
evenings, (again and again),
by men whom neither traffic
nor merchandise can divert
from the Remembrance of
God, nor from regular Prayer
nor from the practice of
regular Charity: their only
fear is for the Day when
hearts and eyes will be
transformed (in a world
wholly new).
    [XXIV : 36-37]

And the places of
worship are for God
(alone): so invoke not
any one along with
God.
    [LXXII : 18]

And that ye set
your whole selves
(to Him) at every
time and place
of prayer, and call
upon Him, making
your devotion sincere
as in His sight:
Such as He created
you in the beginning,
so shall ye return.
    [VII : 29]

O Children of Adam!
wear your beautiful
apparel at
every time and
place of prayer.
    [VII : 31]

Mosques used to function as religious centres for educating, disciplining, guiding and instructing Muslims. In them were resolved social and religious problems of Muslims. Instructions were issued from there to Muslims relating to all important affairs. When an important event occurred and Muslims needed new instructions, the Prophet of Allah, blessings and peace be upon him, ordered that a call (*Salatul Jame'a*) be given signifying that all Muslims (including those usually praying in other mosques and living in distant areas) should gather in the Prophet's mosque for prayer, as a matter of import and consequence was to be discussed there.

Mosques continued to play this important role ever since. Life in a Muslim society used to revolve around them. All endeavours of knowledge and guidance and all movements of reform and welfare arose from them. The present Muslim society has to acknowledge this important role that mosques can play in providing it a positive direction.

Friday Prayer

On Fridays a special congregational prayer called *Salatul Jum'a* (Friday Prayer) is offered instead of the Noon Prayer (*Salatuz Zuhr*). It is offered at the time of the Noon Prayer. In it two *Rak'ahs* are offered as against four *Rak'ahs* offered in the Noon Prayer. Also, unlike the Noon Prayer, it is offered audibly.

Friday Prayer consists of such etiquette, instructions, and qualities which add significantly to its grandeur and create in worshippers a fresh desire and eagerness to sincerely pray to God, try to attain closeness to Him, unify Muslims and generate among them a spirit to help one another in matters of virtue and piety. Allah states in the Quran:

O ye who believe!
when the call is proclaimed
to prayer on Friday
(the Day of Assembly),
hasten earnestly to the
Remembrance of God, and
leave off business (and
traffic): that is best

28

for you if ye but
knew!
    [LXII : 9]

The importance of the Friday Prayer has also been
emphasized in the following Hadith:

Allah seals the heart
of a person who
misses Friday Prayers
for three weeks out
of laziness.

Muslims have been instructed to prepare for Friday Prayer
by taking bath, brushing their teeth with *Miswak* (soft twig
brush), applying perfume, and attaining as much cleanliness as
possible. In Friday Prayer a *Khutha* (sermon) is also delivered
by the Imam. The *Khutbas* delivered by the Prophet, blessings
and peace be on him, were not lifeless, dull or devoid of
message and instruction. Instead, they used to be fully relevant
to the lives of the people and situations of the time.

Muslims are instructed to listen to the *Khutba* quietly and
attentively so that they could fully benefit from the teachings
and instructions contained in it in the serene and spiritual
environment of the mosque. In fact, the *Khutba* is an act of
prayer, not a piece of oration. That is why it is strictly
forbidden for Muslims to talk during the *Khutba*.

Friday Sermon (*Khutba*)

The translation of an Arabic *Khutba* (sermon) is presented below to let the readers have a general understanding of the content, message, and spirit of a typical Friday *Khutba*. This *Khutba* is very popular in India and is recited frequently by *Imams* in Friday Prayers.

"After glorifying Allah and invoking Allah's blessings on the Prophet: 'O people! adopt the principle of *Tawheed* (i.e. believe in Allah as One in His Being and Attributes and do not ascribe any partner to Him), because *Tawheed* is the highest form of faithfulness to Allah and the greatest deed. Show consideration and propriety to Allah as it is the root of all virtuous deeds. Hold strongly to the ways of the Prophet, blessings and peace be on him, because the ways of the Prophet (*Sunnah*) lead one to submission and obedience to Allah, and he who obeys Allah and the Prophet is on the straight path and reaches his destination. Always stay away from innovations (*Bid'ah*), because they lead one to disobedience to Allah ultimately resulting in his going astray.

"Adopt the path of truth throughout your life, because truth leads to deliverance and falsehood causes destruction. Adopt the practice of doing good to others because those who do so are dear to Allah. Never lose hope in the mercy of Allah because He is the Most Merciful. Do not fall in love with the temporal world lest you should lose everything. Remember, nobody meets his death until his last provision in the world has reached him. It is, therefore, futile to try to earn livelihood by disobeying Allah and disregarding Islamic laws differentiating between the allowed and the forbidden, the appropriate and the inappropriate. To achieve your aims adopt only such means which are good.

"Trust in Allah in all your matters because He cares so much for those who repose trust in Him. Do not show slackness in supplicating to Allah because Allah listens to all and accepts their supplications. Keep on asking Him for His forgiveness for your sins and keep on offering repentance to Him; this will create abundance (*Barakah*) in your property and progeny. Allah says in the Quran:

And your Lord says:
"Call on me; I
will answer your
(Prayer): But those
who are too arrogant
to serve Me will
surely find themselves
in Hell--in humiliation.
    [XL : 60]

"May Allah give you and me in abundance from the riches of the Quran and help you and me with its verses and its teachings of wisdom. I pray to Allah to forgive you and me and all other Muslims. You also seek forgiveness from Him. Indeed, He is the Most Forgiving, the Most Merciful."

31

Different Levels of Prayer

Salah (Prayer) is not something static or fixed like an iron or wooden frame which would force all worshippers to remain at one and the same level, disallowing them to rise higher than the ordinary level. It, in fact, enfolds a very wide state of mind, heart and soul in which a worshipper moves on from one level to another: from the ordinary to the advanced, from the advanced to the perfect, and form the perfect to those still higher levels which remain unexplored even by his imagination. In *Salah*, therefore, the status of worshippers differs from one another. How can a *Salah* performed in carelessness and ignorance be equal to a *Salah* marked by concentration and understanding? In the same way, the prayers of the commoner cannot attain the level of excellence marking the prayers of the pious. Also, it is not necessary that a worshipper performs the same level of *Salah* all the time; his *Salah* offered on one day may differ in excellence from his *Salah* offered the day before or the day after.

That is why two kinds of *Salah* are mentioned in the Quran--one marked with Allah's displeasure and the other with His approval. It is stated in the Quran:

So owe to the
worshippers who
are neglectful
of their Prayers,
those who (want but)
to be seen (of men),

but refuse (to supply even)
neighbourly needs.
    [CVII :4-7]

Another kind of *Salah* is thus mentioned in the Quran:

The believers must (eventually)
win through, -- those who
humble themselves in their
prayers.
    [XXIII : 1-27]

Similarly, the Prophet of Allah, blessings and peace be upon him, has also referred to *Salah* as of two kinds: *Salah* performed with due concentration and that done in carelessness. About the first kind, the Prophet, blessings and peace be on him, said:

(The Prophet performed
Wudu (ablution)
and did it well
and then said): "If
a person performs
Wudu like
me, offers two rak'ahs
of Salah, and does
not let any other
thought distract him,
he will be absolved
from all past sins."

About the other kind of *Salah* Ammar Bin Yasir reports the following words of the Prophet, blessings and peace be on him: "A person completes his *Salah* but he gets only the one-tenth of [the reward] of it, and sometimes the one-ninth, the one-eight, the one-seventh, the one-sixth, the one-fifth, the one-fourth, the one-third, or only the one-half" (Abu Dawud and Nassai). The Prophet, blessings and peace be on him, also said, "The worst person is he who steals form his *Salah*." The Companions asked, "O Prophet of Allah, how does one steal from his *Salah*?" The Prophet replied, "He does not perform well either his *Ruku'* (kneeling) or *Sujood* (Prostration)" (Muslim).

The status of persons in regard to their performance in *Salah* differs from one another. The *Salah* of the Prophet of Allah, blessings and peace be on him, was the best, most consummate and perfect, worthy of weighing heaviest in Allah's scale. Abu Bakr's *Salah* had the greatest resemblance to the Prophet's. That is why the Prophet asked Abu Bakr to lead the congregational prayers in his mosque during his sickness and insisted on it although Aisha bint Abu Bakr, may Allah be pleased with her, suggested Umar bin Khattab's name instead.

That is why the status of a person as a Muslim can be determined better by the quality of his *Salah* than by anything else, such as knowledge, intelligence, or academic excellence. The persons whose names remain immortal in Islamic history and who stand so distinguished among their contemporaries were those who strove so sincerely to improve the quality of their *Salah* and to attain the highest level of God-consciousness called in Islamic terminology *Ihsan*.

ZAKAH (Poor-due): Second Pillar of Islam

But (even so), if they
repent, establish
regular prayers,
and practise regular
charity,-- they are
your brethren in Faith.
  [IX : 11]

Importance of *Zakah*

In the Quran *Zakah* (Poor-duè) hass been mentioned together with *Salah* (Prayer) at eighty-two places: a typical instance may be seen in the the verse qouted above. Also, wherever in the Quran the qualities of believers are described, their eagerness for establishing Prayer and Poor-due is mentioned together. The Prophet of Allah, blessings and peace be upon him, has mentioned *Zakah* as a fundamental tenet of Islam. When once asked what Islam was, he replied, "Worship Allah and do not ascribe any partner to Him, establish obligatory *Salah* (Regular Prayers), pay *Zakah* (Poor-due), and observe *Sawm* (Fasting) in Ramadan (Bukhari and Muslim)". Dhammam Bin Tha'laba narrates that once he inquired of the Prophet, "I ask you in the name of Allah whether He has commanded you to collect *Zakah* (Poor-due) from the rich among us and distribute it among the poor?" The Prophet, blessings and peace be upon him, replied, 'certainly'."

The Traditions of the Prophet of Allah, blessings and peace be upon him, in support of the obligatoriness of *Zakah* are very large in number and have been read and believed ever since the lifetime of the Prophet. Muslim scholars are of consensus that *Zakah* is obligatory on Muslims like *Salah* and Muslims have been sincerely observing the pratice of paying *Zakah* throughout the history of Islam. Allah has mentioned performance of *Salah* and giving of *Zakah* as signs of a believer's correct faith, obedience to his Lord, peace with Him, and feeling of brotherhood for Muslims in general. It is stated in the Quran:

But if they repent,
and establish
regular prayers
and practise
regular charity,
then open the way for them:
For God is Oft-forgiving,
Most Merciful.
  [IX : 5]

The same theme is stated again at another place in the Quran in these words:

But (even so), if
they repent, and
establish regular
prayers, and practise
regular charity, --
they are your brethren
in Faith: (Thus) do
We explain the signs
in detail, for those
who understand.
  [IX : 11]

Allah Absolute Owner of All Things

It is a basic principle of Islam's economic system that everything belongs to Allah. The Quran teaches man to submit all his affairs to Allah and emphasizes only one responsibility of man--his vicegerancy of Allah on earth. It addresses Muslims in these words:

Yea, give them
something yourselves
out of the means
which God has
given to you.
[XXIV : 33]

It also presents the same theme in the following way:

And spend (in charity)
out of the (substance) whereof
He has made you heirs.
  [LVII : 7]

It is clearly stated in the above verses that the true owner of all things is Allah. Man, therefore, does not have any right to take pride in having given out as *Zakah* a very small portion of his wealth with which Allah has entrusted him.

And what cause
have ye why ye should
not spend in the cause
of God? -- For to God

belongs the heritage of
the heavens and the
earth.
    [LVII : 10]

Man should, therefore, realize and accept that he is in fact not the master of his belongings, land and property, but merely a trustee answerable to the Supreme Master, Allah the Almighty.

Man Temporal Owner of Property

But Allah, the Wise and the Merciful, does not deprive man of the satisfaction of being the owner of his property which sometimes appears to him as fruit of his efforts. Although denying the right of ownership to man should have been perfectly justified, it would have adversely affected man's self-confidence, enthusiasm, ability to grow, spirit of competitiveness, interest in exploratory enterprises, and, in short, the gratification that he naturally enjoys by considering his earnings as fruit of his labour.

It is the same kind of happiness that man experiences in associating himself to his family home and in enheriting his ancestoral property. If he were denied this happiness, he would have never felt love and gratitude for his predecessors and desire to protect and multiply the property for himself and his successors. Human life then would have lost all marks of enthusiasm, competitiveness, and ambition which are necessary for the existence and advancement of man. The world, then, would have been reduced to a large workshop allowing human beings to move like parts of a machine--deaf, dumb, without heart and conscience, incapable of enjoying contentment or appreciating happiness.

That is why Allah has repeatedly referred to wealth as possession of man, not of the Creator or Provider:

And do not eat up
your property among
yourselves for
vanities, nor use
it as bait for
the judges, with intent
that ye may eat up
wrongfully and knowingly
a little of (other) people's
property.
    [II : 188)

O ye who believe!
give of the good things
which ye have
(honourably) earned, and
of the fruits of the earth
which We have produced
for you.
    [II : 267]

To those weak of
understanding make
not over your property.
    [IV : 5]

Thus, a large number of verses in the Quran do not only refer to wealth as man's possession, but at places mention spending of it for the pleasure of Allah on noble causes as virtuous loan to Allah.

Who is he that will
loan to God a beautiful
loan, which God will
double unto his credit
and multiply many times.
    [II : 245]

Wisdom Behind Fixing Percentage of *Zakah*

As the Islamic society expanded with time, people fell into different economic classes: the rich, the poor, and the average. Also, there lived in that society the highly generous, the extremely miser, and the ones following the middle course. They also differed in the level of faith: persons of strong faith could easily make a great financial sacrifice for the needy while those weak in faith found giving even a little money to others by way of help very trying for themselves.

It was, thus, Allah's great prudence that He Himself fixed for the rich a percentage of their savings as *Zakah* which remains suitable for all people at all times. The percentage of *Zakah* fixed in Islam is neither so large as to strain the middle-class people, nor so little as to appear petty and insignificant to the rich.

Allah did not leave the percentage of *Zakah* to be fixed by individuals on the basis of their individual ambition, for ambitions vary from person to person and from time to time. Even Muslim scholars or Muslim rulers were not entrusted with this task, for they were not above human weaknesses either. Thus, it was indeed the wisdom of Allah that He made *Zakah* obligatory and Himself fixed its percentage to save Muslims from confusion.

Articles for Which *Zakah* Is to Be Paid

The Prophet of Allah, blessings and peace be on him, prescribed the percentage of *Zakah,* mentioned the things for which *Zakah* had to be paid and laid down the conditions in which it became obligatory. He divided such things into four categories: (1) produce of cultivation and garden, (2) cattle (camels, cows, goats, etc.), (3) gold and silver, which are the bases of the whole financial system, and (4) commercial articles of all kinds.

Zakah is obligatory on a Muslim once a year. But for gardening and cultivation, a year's period will be considered as complete only when the fruit in the garden and harvest in the field are ripe and ready. In fact, the period of one year for the payment of *Zakah* was most appropriate and suitable to all. If it were paid monthly or weekly, the rich would have been put under great strain. If it were paid once in lifetime, the poor and the needy would have been hurt.

The percentage of *Zakah* is determined on the basis of the labour and effort involved in managing a particular source of income. For example, if a person finds a treasure by chance, a

41

year's time is not needed to pay *Zakah* on it. He will have to pay one-fifth of it as *Zakah* as soon as he takes possession of it. But if a person makes effort and undertakes labour in manipulating a source of income, he will pay one-tenth, as is the case with the produce of cultivation and gardening. This is so when he cultivates a piece of land by ploughing it and sowing seeds in it himself but not doing anything to irrigate it, as the land is itself irrigated by natural water. But if he is also responsible for irrigating the land, he will pay the twentieth part of the harvest as *Zakah*.

If there is a source of income in which the profit depends on the labour of the owner who is also responsible for its management, administration and security, he will be required to pay the fortieth part of the income only. This is so because in such a business a person remains more responsible for administration, time, and security than a cultivator or a gardener. Similarly, the cultivation done with the help of natural rains is easier than the cultivation done through irrigation. In the same way, the discovery of a treasure is the easiest of all sources of income mentioned above.

Uses of *Zakah*

The uses of *Zakah* are laid down in the following verse of the Quran:

Alms are for the
poor and the needy,
and those employed
to administer the
(funds); for those whose

42

*hearts have been
(recently) reconciled
(to truth); for those
in bondage and in
debt; in the cause
of God; and for the
wayfarer: (Thus it is)
ordained by God, and
God is full of knowledge
and wisdom.*
    [IX : 60]

Zakah a Form of Worship, Not a Penalty

It should be remembered that *Zakah* is not a tax or a penalty imposed by a state. It is an act of worship like *Salah* (Prayers) and *Sawm* (Fasting) and is a means of securing Allah's approval as well as moral discipline and refinement. While paying *Zakah*, therefore, a person should never let any feeling of superiority or pride, such as being in a priveleged position of obliging the poor, rise in his heart. Instead, he should do it with humbleness and, in fact, feel grateful to the poor who accept it. It is required that one should carefully look for and select the deserving recipients of *Zakah* himself. It is also considered better to distribute *Zakah* among the poor of the same place from where it is collected (unless there are no poor people in that area). In the Quran *Zakah* is projected as a deed opposite in nature to interest: interest is condemend as much as *Zakah* is praised.

Giving Away Extra Wealth as Charity

The Prophet of Allah, blessings and peace be on him, tried to create this moral attitude in his Companions and followers that all extra wealth had to be given away to the needy for the pleasure of Allah. For this he invoked them so effectively that people sometimes wondered if they really had any right to keep to themselves their extra wealth. The fact, however, remains that to give away all extra wealth is not a law in Islam, but a virtuous deed done in goodwill that Islam wishes to promote among its adherents. The Prophet of Islam, bleesings and peace be upon him, himself exemplified this quality to the highest degree.

*Ye have indeed in
the Apostle of God a
beautiful pattern (of
conduct) for any one
whose hope is in God
and the Final Day, and
who engages much in the
praise of God.
[XXXIII : 21]*

The Prophet, blessings and peace be upon him, is reported to have said in an Authentic Hadith, "Whoever has an extra animal to ride should give it away to him who doesn't have one. Whoever has an extra breakfast should give it away to him who doesn't have one" (*Abu Dawud*).

The Prophet, blessings and peace be on him, also said, "He who has food for two persons should also invite the third to eat with them. He who has food for three should also invite the fourth" (*Tirmidhi*).

The Prophet, blessings and peace be on him, also said, "He did not bear faith in me who ate to his fill and slept all night knowing that his neighbour was starting" (*Tabrani*).

It is related in another Tradition that a man came to the Prophet of Allah, blessings and peace be on him, and said, "O Prophet of Allah, give me some clothes to wear". The Prophet enquired, "Don't you have any neighbour who has some extra pairs of clothes?" The man replied, "There are more than one [such persons]." The Prophet said thereupon, "May Allah not join you and them then in the paradise" (*Tabrani*).

Value of Man in Islam

Prophet Muhammad, blessings and peace be on him, elevated the position of human being and value of human sympathy and compassion to a height which was beyond human imagination. According to the teachings of Islam, if a person fails to sympathize and support an aggrieved person, he is like one who fails in obeying Allah. The following saying of the Prophet, which is a Divine Tradition (*Hadith Qudsi*), underscores this theme very effectively.

"Allah will tell one of His bondsmen on the Day of Judgement, 'I fell ill, but you did not visit Me'. He will reply, 'Lord! how could have I visited You, for You are the Cherisher and Sustainer of the worlds?' Allah will tell him, 'Didn't you know that such and such slave of Mine was ill, but you did not visit him. Had you visited him, you would have found Me there. O son of Adam! I asked you for food but you did not give food to Me'. He will submit, 'My Sustainer and Cherisher, how could have I provided You with food, for You Yourself are the Cherisher and Sustainer of the worlds?' Allah will tell him, 'Don't you remember that such and such slave of Mine asked you for food, but you did not give food to him. Had you given food to him, it would have reached Me. O son of Adam, I asked you for water but you did not give Me water to drink.' He will submit again, 'Lord! how could have I given You water to drink, for You are the Cherisher and Sustainer of the worlds?' Allah will tell him, 'Such and such bondsman of Mine asked you for water but you did not give him water to drink. Had you given him water to drink, you would have found it with Me' (Muslim)."

This is, indeed, the highest level of Allah's appreciation of a person's help to his fellow beings. There is yet another Tradition in which the Prophet, blessings and peace be on him, has emphasized the value of having compassion and goodwill for one another:

"None of you could
be a perfect believer
unless he wishes for
his brother [in faith]
what he wishes for
himself."

SAWM (Fasting): Third Pillar

Commandment for Fasting

The divine commandment for Fasting was revealed after the *Hijrah* (Emigration from Makkah to Madinah) when Muslims were relieved of oppression, poverty and indigence that they had experienced in Makkah and started living in Madinah in ease and comfort. Had the order for Fasting (*Sawm*) been given at Makkah, people might have related it to the Muslim's resourcelessness and stringency during their stay there. They could have developed a feeling that Fasting was for the poor, the indigent, the sufferer, and the oppressed and that the rich and the well-to-do, the owners of the gardens and lands were, perhaps, not the real addressees of this commandment.

The verses of the Quran which contain the order for Fasting as an obligatory duty for Muslims are as follows:

O ye who believe! Fasting
is prescribed to you as it
was prescribed to those
before you, that ye may (learn)
self-restraint.
(Fasting) for a fixed number
of days; but if any of you is
ill, or in a journey, the prescribed
number (should be made up) from
days later. For those who can
do it (with hardship), is a
ransom, the feeding of one that
is indigent. But he that will give

47

more, of his own free will, --
it is better for him, and it
is better for ye that ye
fast, if ye only knew.

Ramadhan is the (month) in
which was sent down the Quran,
as a guide to mankind, also
clear (signs) for guidance and
judgement (between right and
wrong). So every one of you who
is present (at his home) during
that month should spend it in
fasting, but if any one is ill,
or on a journey, the prescribed
period (should be made up)
by days later. God intends
every facility for you; He
does not want to put you
to difficulties. (He wants you)
to complete the prescribed
period, and to glorify
Him in that He has
guided you; and perchance
ye shall be grateful.
    [II : 183-85]

These verses, which announce the obligatoriness of Fasting
(*Sawm*) for the first time, do not lay down dry laws concerning
Fasting which may be noticed in the case of man-made laws
existing, for example, between the citizens and the ruler of a

state. They, instead, appeal to the belief and faith, reason and conscience, heart and soul at one and the same time and prepare Muslims to take the commandment for Fasting as a most welcome tenet of religion, not as a dictate of law. This is, in fact, an undeniable miracle of the Quran's principles of calling to the Truth and its ability to formulate prudent and psychologically sound laws.

It is sent down by One
full of wisdom, worthy of
all praise.
　[XLI : 42]

The objective of Fasting is to discipline and reform the believers, not to put them to hardship. Fasting, in fact, serves as a medium of moral training helping Muslims to rise to a level of moral and spiritual perfection where they learn to control their desires and deal as masters with them, not as slaves. If they develop a moral strength to give up desirable things such as cool water and tasteful food from dawn to dusk to observe Fasting, will they not then try to stay away from things forbidden by Allah?

Virtues of Fasting

Fasting, as enunciated in Islam, is perfect as an act of worship both in laws and objectives and reflects the great wisdom of Allah, the Most Powerful, the Knowing, the Wise.

Should He not know--
He that created? And
He is the One that understands

the finest mysteries (and) is
well-acquainted (with them).
[LXVII : 14]

The virtues of Fasting are elaborately mentioned in the following Tradition:

"Abu Huraira reports that the Prophet of Allah said, ' The deed of a son of Adam is increased several times (in Ramadan) and the reward is increased by ten times to seven hundred times. Allah says that Fasting is specially for Him and He Himself will deliver its rewards (to His bondsman) as he abstains from eating and controls his desires only for Him. There are (two instances of) happiness for the fasting Muslim: one is at the time of breaking his fast and the other at the tim of meeting his Lord. And verily to Allah the smell of a fasting person's breath is the best and cleanest?"

In another Tradition the Prophet has mentioned the rewards of Fasting in this way:

"Sahal bin S'ad relates from the Prophet of Allah, blessings and peace be on him, ' There is a door of Paradise called *Rayyan* toward which only the Fasting will be called. Only the Fasting will enter it and those who enter it will never feel thirsty."

Wisdom in Associating Fasting with Ramadan

Allah has ordained Muslims to fast in the specific month of Ramadan and has thus made Fasting and Ramadan dependent on each other. Udoubtedly this union of the two sources of blessings contains great wisdom and importance. Most importantly, it is the month of Ramadan in which the Quran was revealed and, thus, humanity was blessed with the brightness of the daybreak of the divine guidance. It is, therefore, most appropriate that as the beginning of Fasting is tied up with daybreak, fasting for an entire month should also be tied up with the month of Ramadan which (due to the revelation of the Quran in it) marks the birth of a morning after a long and dark night of ignorance. In addition, as the month of Ramadan was richer than all other months in Allah's mercy and favour and in spiritual environment, it deserved well that its days were further adorned with Fasting and its nights with acts of worship.

There is a very intimate and special relationship between Fasting and the Quran. That is why the Prophet of Allah, blessings and peace be upon him, used to recite the Quran with greater interest and eagerness in the month of Ramadan. Ibn Abbas relates, " The Prophet of Allah, blessings and peace be upon him, was the most generous of all, but in Ramadan, when Jibrail visited him [regularly], his generosity increased more than ever. Jibrail used to visit him every night in Ramadan and go over the Quran with him. In those days when Jibrail used to meet him, he became faster than the fast-blowing wind in generosity, bestowal, and other virtuous deeds" (Agreed).

Ramadan: A Global Season of Worship and Good Deeds

All these things have made Ramadan a global season and a time of grand celebration of worship, God-remembrance, recitation of the Quran, self-restraint, and piety in which Muslims--educated and uneducated, rich and poor, humble and priveleged--participate like close friends and associates all over the world. Ramadan falls at the same time in every city, town, and village in the world. Its arrival can be noticed equally in the palaces of the rich as well as huts of the poor. No one can dare do its rituals differently according to his personal understanding, nor is there any scope for a disagreement in determining the number of its days. The grandeur and beauty of Ramadan is, in fact, easily noticeable throughout the length and breadth of the Muslim world. It seems as if a canopy of effulgence and peace is raised all over the Muslim society. Even those who are slack in Fasting choose to fast in Ramadan for the fear of being alienated in the Muslim community. If for some reason they decide not to fast, they eat in the day hiding from others in shame. The sick and the traveller are, of course, lawfully exempted from Fasting. Fasting is thus observed collectively throughout the world in the same month. This creates a congenial and conducive atmosphere for the believers due to which Fasting becomes easy, hearts soften, and Muslims turn to deeds of worship and submission, sympathy and compassion with greater eagerness.

Pre-Dawn Meal (*Sahoor*)

At night, before the daybreak, Muslims take some food in order to keep up their energy for Fasting in the day (so that hunger and thirst do not become intolerable). This meal is called *Sahoor* in Islamic terminology. This is a *Sunnah* and the Prophet of Allah, blessings and peace be on him, has encouraged Muslims to observe this practice. Anas bin Malik relates that the Prophet of Allah said, "Take *Sahoor* because there is amplitude (*Barakah*) in it" (*Bukhari, Muslim, Tirmidhi, & Nassai*). In another Tradition Amr bin al-'As

52

relates that the Prophet of Allah, blessings and peace be on him, said, " The difference between our Fasting and that of the *Ahle-Kitah* (People of the Book) is marked by *Sahoor* (Pre-Dawn Meal)" (Muslim).

The Prophet of Allah, blessings and peace be on him, has also forbidden Muslims from delaying breaking of fast and has mentioned it to be a sign of disgression and a mark of the extremists among the *Ahle-Kitah* (People of the Book). Suhail bin S'ad relates that the Prophet of Allah, blessings and peace be on him, said, " So long as Muslims keep on breaking fast without delay, they will remain on (the path of) virtue" (*Bukhari, Muslim, Muatta, Tirmidhi*).

The Prophet, blessings and peace be upon him, used to break fast before the evening prayers (*Salatul Maghrib*). If juicy dates were available, he ate some of them; otherwise, he took dry dates. If dates were not available, he drank some water. He used to say the following words at the time of breaking fast:

O Allah! I observed
fast for you and I
break fast with the
provision granted by
You.

He also used to add these words:

The thirst is
satiated, the
veins become
wet and, God-willing,
the reward is certain.

Safeguarding the Spirit of Fasting

The Islamic Shari'a does not address itself only to the physical etiquette of Fasting; it also pays full attention to its real aim and spirit. It has made unlawful not only eating, drinking, and sexual relationship during the period of Fasting, but has also forbidden the believers from all such things which defeat the noble aims of Fasting and destroy its spiritual and moral benefits. It has circumscribed Fasting with discipline, piety, cleanliness and sincerity of heart and tongue. The Prophet of Allah, blessings and peace be on him, once said, "If any one of you is fasting, he should not indulge in abusive and useless talk, nor should he turn noisy creating disturbance. If someone calls him names and picks up a quarrel with him, he should tell him that he is Fasting." The Prophet, blessings and peace be upon him, also said, "He who does not give up telling lies and practising upon them (should know that) Allah has no need that he should renounce eating and drinking."

The act of Fasting, if devoid of sincerety and piety, is like a form without reality, a body without soul. The Prophet of Allah, blessings and peace be on him, once emphasized this point in these words: "There are many fasting people who do not earn from their fast anything except thirst, as there are devotees who do not get from their nocturnal prayers (*Tahajjud*) anything except vigil at night" (*Bukhari*). A Muslim has to safeguard the form as well as the spirit of Fasting. The Prophet, blessings and peace be on him, emphasized the same point in these words: "Fasting is a shield until it is torn asunder."

Fasting in Islam is not merely a command forbidding Muslims from eating and drinking, backbiting and aspersing, quarreling and cursing; it also encourages Muslims in a truly positive vein to learn to live a virtuous life and perform virtuous deeds. Ramadan is, therefore, the most suitable time for engaging oneself in good deeds, such as prayers and recitation of the Quran, remembrance and glorification of Allah, and sympathizing with and helping the needy and the poor. The Prophet of Allah, blessings and peace be on him, has said, "If a person tries to win Allah's pleasure with a virtuous deed in it (Ramadan), his deed will be considered equal to an obligatory deed (*Fard*) performed in days other than Ramadan. And if a person performs an obligatory deed (*Fard*) in this month, his deed will be equal to seventy such obligatory deeds performed in days other than Ramadan. This is the month of patience and the reward of patience is paradise. This is the month of sympathy."

Zaid bin Khalid Al-Johani reports the Prophet of Allah, blessings and peace be on him, as saying, "He who feeds a fasting person at the time of breakfast will get a reward equal to that of the fasting person, and the reward of the person fasting will not be reduced."

Also, Allah has blessed the Muslim Ummah throughout the world with an eagerness and enthusiasm to observe the practice of offering special Ramadan prayers at night called *Salatut Taraweeh*. Scholars agree to it that the Prophet of Allah, blessings and peace be on him, offered *Salatut Taraweeh*. He discontinued performing it after three days lest it should be made obligatory on Muslims and be tiring for them.

All these points have made Ramadan a festival of worship, a season of recitation of the Quran, and an occassion of exultation and rejoice for the pious and the virtuous. In this month Muslims distinctly exhibit a remarkably increased attachment to religion, love for Allah, and eagerness to compete with one another in performing good deeds.

Seclusion (*E'tekaf*)

Seclusion in the mosque (*E'tekaf*) in Ramadan in its last ten days is a deed bearing great rewards. It is a *Sunnah* (Prophetic tradition) very dear to Muslims and a deed safeguarding for them the benefits of Ramadan and accomplishment of its objectives. During *E'tekaf* Muslims engage themselves in good deeds, such as prayers, recitation of the Quran, remembrance of Allah, ffering repentence, and invoking Allah's blessings and peace on the Prophet. The Prophet of Allah, blessings and peace be on him, observed *E'tekaf* regularly every year, and afterward the Muslims throughout the world have very sincerely adhered to this practice. *E'tekaf*, therefore, has become a feature of Ramadan and gained the status of a Continued Prophetic Tradition (*Sunnah Mutawatir*). It is related by Aisha, may Allah be pleased with her, that "the Prophet of Allah, blessings and peace be upon him, used to observe *E'tekaf* in every Ramadan in its last ten days until he departed from the world. After him his (rightly guided) wives kept alive the practice of *E'tekaf*" (Agreed). It is related on the authority of Abu Hurraira, may Allah be pleased with him, that "the Prophet of Allah, blessings and peace be upon him, used to observe *E'tekaf* every Ramadan in its last ten days. He observed *E'tekaf* for twenty days in the year in which he passed away" (Bukhari).

Night of Power (*Lailatul Qadr*)

The great value of the Night of Power (*Lailatul Qadr*) has been emphasized in the Quran and in the Traditions of the Prophet, blessings and peace be on him, at various places. At one place in the Quran a whole chapter is devoted to this theme:

We have indeed
revealed this (Message)
in the Night of Power:
And what will
explain to thee what
the Night of Power is?

The Night of Power
is better than a thousand
months.

Therein come down the
angels and the Spirit
by God's permission,
on every errand:

Peace!...This until
the rise of morn!
[XCVII : 1-5]

The Prophet, blessings and peace be on him, is reported to have said, "The past sins of a person who remains engaged in acts of worship in the Night of Power with faith and awareness of Reckoning will be forgiven" (Agreed).

It is, indeed, Allah's wisdom and kindness that He has left this night unidentified and has simply referred to it as one falling in the last ten days of Ramadan. This, as a matter of fact, encourages Muslims to adorn all the last ten nights of Ramadan with acts of worship, supplication and invocation in search of this night, as the Prophet, blessings and peace be on him, himself used to do. Aisha, may Allah be pleased with her, narrates: "During the last ten days of Ramadan, the Prophet of Allah, blessings and peace be on him, used to stay awake all night, wake up the members of his family too, and become alert and enthusiastic" (Agreed).

Most Traditions agree that *Lailatul Qadr* falls in the last ten days of Ramadan, probably in the last seven days, and is one of the odd nights. Ibn Umar narrates, "*Lailatul Qadr* was shown in dream to some of the Companions of the Prophet as occurring in the last seven days [of Ramadan]. On it the Prophet, blessings and peace be on him, remarked that as their dreams were mostly in agreement about the last seven days, those wishing to find it should search for it in the last seven days." Aisha, may Allah be pleased with her, narrates, "The Prophet of Allah, blessings and peace be on him, used to observe seclusion in the mosque (*E'tekaf*) in Ramadan in its last ten days and told (us) to search for *Lailatul Qadr* in the last ten days of Ramadan." In another Tradition related again by Aisha, may Allah be pleased with her, the Prophet of Allah, blessings and peace be on him, said: "Search *Lailatul Qadr* in the odd nights of the last ten days of Ramadan" (*Bukhari*).

Moon of Eid Marking the End of Ramadan

Time passes fast and the month of Ramadan comes to an end quicker than expected. The eagerness of the believers for offering devotional services and attaining spiritual excellence was not yet satiated, the call rising from their hearts still demanded "More, can I have more of Ramadan", and even the commoners were becoming increasingly attached to Fasting that the moon of the next month rises in the sky. With it the month of Ramadan bids farewell to Muslims with a promise to come again next year. With the sight of the moon of the new month the hearts of Muslims are filled with thankfulness marked with patience replacing patience marked with thankfulness that they experienced in Ramadan. One guest and messenger of Allah, Ramadan, bade farewell to Muslims but another guest and messenger, Eid, arrives in its place. Yesterday it was forbidden to eat in the day; tomorrow it will be forbidden to abstain from food. That was the order of Allah and this is the order of Allah as well.

HAJJ (Pilgrimage): Fourth Pillar

Hajj (Pilgrimage) is the fourth pillar of Islam. If a Muslim does not perform *Hajj* in spite of his ability to perform it, he may be considered a renegade according to some Quranic verses and Traditions. This obligatory deed is performed at Makkah al-Mukarramah in Saudi Arabia in specified days of a specific lunar month.

Relevance of Prophet Ibrahim's Story to Hajj

Prophet Ibrahim (Abraham) was a son of an idol-maker who was also a priest at the largest centre of worship in his home city. Thus both by profession as well as faith, he was strongly committed to the worship centre he was associated with. This was a difficult situation because if faith is coupled with material gain, the attachment becomes more rigid and uncompromising. There was nothing in that environment which would have created in Prophet Ibrahim's heart faith in and love for One God and persuaded him to revolt against the prevailing polytheistic way of life. But Prophet Ibrahim whose noble heart was prepared to shine with the light of prophethood and who was destined to work for creating a new world had to act in a different way:

We bestowed aforetime
on Abraham his rectitude
of conduct, and well were
We acquainted with him.
   [XXI : 51]

Prophet Ibrahim began his revolution from a place where
sometimes even great revolutions of the world did not have an
access. This was his family life -- a place where a person is
born and raised and where he wishes to live all his life. Then
all those incidents came to pass which have been narrated in
the Quran clearly and effectively. They included Prophet
Ibrahim's breaking down the idols, rage of the priests over it
multiplied with surprise and helplessness, their revengefulness
against Prophet Ibrahim, their making a fire for him, the fire
becoming cool on him, and his bold and eloquent dialogue
with the tyrant king of the time.

Prophet Ibrahim's revolt reached a stage where the whole
city turned against him. The government also became hostile
and tried to hurt him. But he remained unimpressed, as if he
expected such repercussions. Calm and contented, he migrated
from his city and began his journey alone and helpless, with
faith in Allah as his only support. Wherever he went, he saw
the same type of human beings and found the same evils of
idol-worship, polytheism, ignorance and slavery to desires
from which he had escaped. He reached Egypt where he faced
a great trial and suffered from an insulting experience as the
ruler there developed an immoral inclination toward his wife.
But he was able to leave Egypt with his wife unhurt. He then
reached Syria and found it hospitable and suitable for his stay.

He decided to stay there and began his work of denouncing the practice of idol-worship and calling people toward the Oneness of Allah.

In Syria which was rich in greenery, means of provision, and beauty of nature, Prophet Ibrahim felt comfortable and at home, but soon he was commanded by Allah to move toward a new country which was sharply opposite to Syria due to its severe climate and formidable natural setting. He was not his own master; his heart was not attached to any specific land, no matter how rich and beautiful it was. He was Allah's slave and His messenger For him the whole world was his homeland and the whole human race was his family. He, therefore, gladly got ready and migrated to Saudi Arabia from Syria with his wife Hajra (Hagar) and his son Ismail.

Allah further ordered him to leave alone his wife and child in a specific valley which was surrounded by barren hills burnt with extreme hot climate. The place had no water which is necessary for sustaining life and looked so awesome with a heavy silence hanging over it. There was no friend or well-whiser around whose presence could have been a source of comfort for him. He had to leave his weak wife and new born child alone there simply because it was Allah's order and did so with full trust in Allah's mercy and power. He was expected not to manifest any hesitation or fear at that time. Ibrahim, may Allah be pleased with him, obeyed the order of Allah with prophetic grace, showing complete disregard for natural resources necessary for survival and reposing all trust in Allah, the Unseen, the Omnipotent.

After Prophet Ibrahim left his family alone in the valley, the child became restless with thirst, but there was no water around, not even in ditches which sometimes contained some water. The mother felt alarmed for the child's safety and restlessly ran between two hills, Safa and Marwa, in search of water. When she reached the second hill, she thought of her child left out unattended and ran back to the first hill to be able to see the child from there and make sure that he was safe. Then again, pressed by her child's urgent need for water, she ran to the second hill hoping that she might find a traveller there or a sign leading to water. Although she was wife of a prophet and mother of a Prophet-to-be, she adopted necessary means to solve her problem and did not consider it an act against the spirit of her trust in Allah.

No doubt, she was restless but her faith in Allah remained unflinching. The scene was truly unique and unprecendented. Then Allah's mercy came to her rescue and miraculously a fountain welled up there, which was later called *Zamzam*. This auspicious source of water flows ceaselessly since then. It never dries out nor does it show any sign of decrease in its water stock. It is used by people throughout the world and generation after generation until today people have been getting water from it profusely. Allah has granted this water abundance and power to cure and sustain. To drink this water also carries reward.

Allah made this act of a sincere believing woman, running between Safa and Marwa, an obligatory condition for *Hajj* for alll pilgrims, whether they were scholars, philosophers, or emperors. Unless they walk briskly between the two hills, which called *Sa'i* in Islamic terminology, their *Hajj* is not complete. The *Sa'i* very appropriately symbolizes the ideal life style of a true believer because it embodies both reason and emotion, feeling and faith. A Muslim makes use of his reason for fulfilling the needs of his life, but at times he also submits to his emotions which are, in fact, rooted more deeply in him than even the reason. He lives in a world full of adornments and attractions, but, following the example of a believer performing *Sai* between the hills of Safa and Marwa in Makkah al-Mukarramah, he keeps on moving without getting distracted by one thing or the other or stopping unduly at a place. His eyes are set on his destination and he is solely concerned about his future. He considers his life as a few rounds of *Sa'i* that he makes in obedience to his Lord following the precedence of his predecessors. His faith does not interfere in his quest for knowledge and exploration and his *Sa'i* does not disturb his trust in Allah. The true value, spirit, and message of *Sa'i* may be expressed in two words: love and submission.

Now the child grew up to the age where his father naturally developed greater attachment to him. The child went out with his father, played happily with him and hung around him all the time. His father, who was specially gifted with compassion and love, got very much attached to the child. This excessive love for the child, however, created a problem for the father. His heart was not an ordinary man's heart. It was the heart of a "Friend of Allah" (*Khalilur Rahman*) which was apt to be a seat of love exclusively for the Almighty Allah. Love, human or divine, can not tolerate a sharer. Thus Allah gave Prophet Ibrahim an indication in dream to sacrifice his beloved son for Him. As a Prophet's dream is like a revelation, Prophet Ibrahim did not fail to understand the will of his Lord and got ready to act accordingly. He first tested his son because it was certainly difficult to perform this task without his cooperation, patience, and forebearance. The son showed the highest level of worthiness, nobility, and submission to the will of the Lord; after all, he was a prophet's son, a future prophet, and a future grandfather of a prophet:

He said: "O my son!
I see in vision that
I offer thee in sacrifice:
Now see what is thy
view!" (The son) said:
"O my father! Do as
thou art commanded:
Thou will find me,
if God so wills, one
practising patience
and constancy!"
[XXXVII : 102]

Whatever happened after that defied all norms of reason. The father went out with his beloved and worthy son to sacrifice him at the command of his Lord. The son followed his father in obedience. Both of them had one and the same goal--to carry out the will of their Lord in perfect submission. The Devil met them in the way and, as he always tries to beguile the virtuous, made an attempt to dissuade them from doing that noble deed. He tried to persuade them in a highly sympathetic and attractive way to disobey Allah. But they refused to listen to him and remained steadfast in their decision to carry out the divine command.

Then came the moment which made the angels, jinns, and human beings restless. Prophet Ibrahim laid his son on the ground and put the knife on his son's throat with a view to sacrifice him in the name of Allah. It was at that time that the mighty will of Allah interfered. The aim behind the whole incident was not to take the life of Ismail. It was, in fact, Prophet Ibrahim's undue love for him, which could have distracted him from loving his Lord most, which was to be sacrificed. When this aim was fulfilled, Allah sent a sheep from the paradise to be slaughtered instead. Allah also established the act of slaughtering an animal as a religous ritual to be practised by the followers of Prophet Ibrahim and all succeeding generations of believers. This is what we notice on the Day of Slaughtering in *Hajj*.

So when they had
both submitted their
wills (to God),
and he had laid
him prostrate on
his forehead
(for sacrifice),
We called out to
him, "O Abraham!
thou hast already
fulfilled the vision!
thus indeed do We
reward those who
do right.

For this was obviously
a trial--and We
ransomed him with
a momentous sacrifice:
And We left (this blessing)
for him among generations
(to come) in later times:
Peace and salutation
to Abraham!"
  [XXXVII : 103-09]

Allah immortalized Prophet Ibrahim's resistence to the beguiles of Satan and commanded the believers to stone the Satan at the places where the Satan had stopped the righteous father and son in an attempt to persuade them not to obey their Lord. The act of stoning, therefore, is done every year in the most auspicious days of *Hajj*. Its main purpose is that Muslims should develop hatred for Satan and show repulsion to him. This is an act in which a believer feels great pleasure provided his faith is strong, understanding correct, and desire to obey the Lord sincere. When he acts the part played by the hero of the story, Prophet Ibrahim, he feels as if he is at war with the forces of the evil, the Satan and his legion, in a battlefield although he understands that stoning does not inflict on the Satan any physical harm save insult and humuliation.

Time moved on. The child attained adulthood and was blessed with the honour of prophethood and leadership. The message preached by Prophet Ibrahim, on the other side, had also spread far and wide. The need of the time then was to establish a religious centre which could be fully trusted by the people and provide strength to the true faith. The world at that time had many palaces for kings and temples for idols, but there was not a single place devoted to Allah exclusively for His worship. That was why when the true religion had been established and a community of Muslims had come into existence, Prophet Ibrahim was commanded by Allah to construct a centre of worship called "the House of Allah" (*Baitullah*). This House was intended to be a place of refuge and peace for the whole humanity in which Allah, the One and the Only God, was worshipped. The worthy father and the worthy son, thus, constructed that auspicious House which was very simple in appearance but very magnificent in appeal. They carried stones and raised the walls of the House:

And remember Abraham
and Ismail raised
the foundations of the
House (with the prayer):
"Our Lord! accept
(this service) from
us: for thou art
the All-Hearing,
the All-Knowing.
Our Lord! make of us
Muslims, bowing to Thy
(Will), and of our
progeny a people
Muslim, bowing to Thy
(Will); and show us
our places for the
celebration of (due) rites;
and turn unto us (in Mercy);

for Thou art the Oft-Returning,
Most Merciful."
    (II : 127-28]

This House was constructed with the highest level of faith and sincerity to serve and please Allah. He accepted it, bestowed it with permanence, beauty and grandeur, turned the hearts of people toward it, and made it a centre for all Muslims to face in prayers. To it the hearts of Muslims were attracted with magnetic effect where Muslims came with utmost eagerness and for which they were willing even to sacrifice their lives. This House was free from all apparent decorations and embellishments and was situated in a town away from the streams of modern civilization. Yet, it had an attraction due to which Muslims lovingly came to it to catch a glipmse of it. When this House was ready, Prophet Ibrahim was instructed thus:

And proclaim the
Pilgrimage among
men: They will
come to thee on
foot and (mounted)
on every kind of
camel, lean on
account of journeys
through deep and
distant mountain
highways; that
they may witness
the benefits (provided)

for them, and celebrate
the name of God, through
the Days appointed,
over the cattle which
He has provided for
them (for sacrifice):
then eat ye thereof
and feed the distressed
ones in want.

Then let them complete
the rites prescribed
for them, perform their
vows, and (again)
circumambulate the
Ancient House.
  [XXII : 27-29]

In the days of Prophet Ibrahim, people were slaves to material resources and valued them as if they were self-existent and independent. Such resources, therefore, ultimately emerged in the society as deities worthy of worship creating a new kind of faith for the people along with their existing faith in idol-worship. The message of Prophet Ibrahim was, in fact, a revolt against idol-worship and worship of all false deities. He called people to worship Allah, the One and the Only God worthy of worship. It was a proclamation of the faith that Allah alone brought all things from non-existence to life. He created things that served human beings as resources and He was their Master. At His will He could deprive a thing of its inherent quality and make it function in the opposite way. He commanded absolute power to use a thing as He wished.

70

Then at a point people made a large fire to burn Ibrahim and said:

Burn him and
protect your gods,
if ye do (anything at all)!
    [XXI : 68]

But Prophet Ibrahim knew well that the fire, like all other things, obeyed Allah's command when it acted. He knew that to burn was not an inseperable quality of fire and that Allah could turn a fire into a garden if He so willed. Prophet Ibrahim, therefore, entered the fire trusting that Allah could protect him even in the fire. When he did so, Allah changed the fire to a garden by His absolute power:

We said. "O Fire!
Be thou cool, and
(a means of) safety
for Abraham!"
Then they sought a
stratagem against
him: but We made
them the ones that
lost most!
    [XXI : 69-70]

It was commonly believed in those days that life was dependent on abundant water, fertile land, and rich gardens. People, therefore, were always in search of such places to settle which were agriculturally rich and commercially promising. Prophet Ibrahim evolted against this materialistic way of thinking and chose for his family such a barren valley for permanent residence which had no agricultural or commercial opportunities. It was a place far from the then commercial centres in the area and was not connected with them by regular roads. After settling down with his family there, Prophet Ibrahim prayed to his Lord to increase their provision, turn the hearts of people toward them, and provide them with fruits of different kinds through His unknown resources.

> *"O our Lord!*
> *I have made*
> *some of my offspring*
> *to dwell in a valley*
> *without cultivation, by*
> *Thy Sacred House;*
> *in order, O our Lord,*
> *that they may establish*
> *regular Prayer: so fill*
> *the hearts of some among*
> *men with love towards*
> *them, and feed them*
> *with fruits: so that*
> *they may give thanks"*
> *[XIV : 37]*

Allah accepted his prayers, made available all kinds of fruit in that town, and blessed it with peace and security.

Have We not
established for them
a secure sanctuary,
to which are brought
as tribute fruits of
all kinds, --a
provision from Ourselves?
But most of them
understand not.
  [XXVIII : 67]

Prophet Ibrahim placed his family at such a place where there was no water even to wet the throat. But Allah brought forth from that land of sand and rock a spring of water which continues to flow to this day, satiates thirst of millions of people, and is carried far and wide throughout the world by the pilgrims.

He left his family at such a desolate and uninhabited place where there was no soul to be seen, but in a short time the place was populated and became a centre of attraction for people from all over the world. The life of Prophet Ibrahim, thus, was a challenge against the excessive dependence on material resources and symbolized comeplte reliance on the absolute power of Allah. In fact, this is an established practice of Allah: He always makes the true faith win over faith in material resources and, if He so wills, produces from such resources results contrary to their nature and, thus, unimaginable by human mind.

HAJJ Reminder of Prophet Ibrahim's Mission

Hajj and its rituals--*Ihram*, the special dress for the occasion, staying in Arafat, circumambulating the K'aba, stoning the Satan, walking between the hills of Safa and Marwa in *Sa'i*--are all, in fact, ways to manifest faith in the Oneness of Allah, negate the undue importance of resources, renew trust in Allah, and strive to attain His pleasure. *Hajj* is an open revolt against false traditions, customs and practices and is an occasion for Muslims to revive faith in Allah and learn to live a life of sacrifice and selflessness. *Hajj* guaranteees cultivation and preservance of such high aims, healthy emotions, noble spiritual and religious values, and selfless human and Islamic brotherhood which are stronger than any nationalistic or geographical ties. It is a call to follow the ways of Prophet Ibrahim, inculcate in oneself his true missionary spirit, and keep up the banner of his mission in all times and climes.

It is the cult of your
father Abraham; It
is He Who has
named you Muslims.
[XXII : 78]

Every year a good number of religious scholars and pious and God-fearing people perform *Hajj* due to whose presence the environment of *Hajj* is deeply charged with spiritual effulgence. This environment moves the hearts even of the hard-hearted; the transgressors return to their Lord in repentance seeking His forgiveness; he eyes which never get

74

wet shed tears profusely for the fear of Allah. The dead and forgetful hearts are revived with new life. The mercy of Allah descends on the pilgrims, peace and tranquility enshrouds the whole environment, and the Satan finds no place to hide his face in shame. It is related in a Hadith: "The Satan is not seen more humiliated and disgraced, rejected and enraged on any day other than the Day of Arafa, and this is because he himself sees that the mercy of Allah i.. descending (on the pilgrims) and that Allah is forgiving (the ir) major sins" (narrated by Malik: *Mursal*).

The environment at the time of *Hajj* has a special effect. It seems as if it is charged with some kind of current. The pilgrims coming from different places to perform *Hajj* find thier hearts once again enlightened with true faith. They are blessed there with faith in Allah, pride in Islam, and true knowledge and understanding of the religion which they take back with them and from which they derive strength to face all kinds of negative persuasion, pressure, temptation and fear that they may encounter later. After returning to their countries they share these blessings of *Hajj* with those who for some reason were not able to perform *Hajj* with them. Thus, a current of faith runs through the whole body of the Muslim Ummah and creates in the ignorant desire to learn, in the weak and meek courage, and in the despondent and depressed enthusiasm and zeal. From it Muslims gather new strength to do the work of preaching. Thus, a new morning is born.

HAJJ Manifestation of Islamic Brotherhood

Hajj is a practical manifestation, proclamation, and victory of Islamic nationalism, if we can use this term, over linguistic and geopraphical nationalism to which many Muslim countries have fallen a prey (due to different factors). In *Hajj* all pilgrims discard their national dresses and put on an Islamic dress called *Ihram* in Islamic terminology. All pilgrims thereafter loudly pronounce together the same words in the same language and in the same spirit:

I am present, O Allah!
I am present. There
is no partner unto
You. All praise and
virtues are for You
as is sovereignty. You
have no partner (indeed).

Among pilgrims there is no differentiation between the ruler and the ruled, the master and the servant, the rich and the poor, the privileged and the unprivileged. They show no difference in the dress they wear or words of *Talbiya* they utter (mentioned above). This is also true about other deeds, rituals, and places relating to *Hajj* in which people of different nationalities stand side by side. They all run between the hills of Safa and Marwa, go together to Mina and then to Arafat, supplicate together at the *Jabale-Rahmah* (Mount of Mercy) in Arafat, and spend the following night together in Muzdalifa. On returning from Muzdalifa they stay in Mina together and together they perform all other rituals of *Hajj,* such as sacrificing an animal, shaving the head, and stoning the Satan. They all move together, stop together, and return together from *Hajj.*

The un-Islamic missions and philosophy of nationalism will not be able to devour Muslims until *Hajj* continues as a living practice among Muslims (and, God-willing, it will always remain so). Also, Muslims will never succeed in constructing a new K'aba in their countries (due to their natural love for their motherland) and promoting it among believers as a site of pilgrimage. The present Centre of Islam, the *Qibla*, will remain unchanged toward which all Muslims in the world turn their faces in prayers. The House of Allah *(Baitullah)* will remain the same to which pilgrims from different parts of the world will keep on travelling for *Hajj*.

*Remember We made
the House a place of
assembly for men
and a place for
safety; and take
ye the station of
Abraham as a
place of prayer.
[II : 125]*

Muslims from far and remote parts of the world will always eagerly try to reach Makkah for *Hajj*, pray vehemently for an opportunity to visit it, and consider it a great fortune if they reach this town.

HAJJ Associated with Specific Time and Place

The rituals of *Hajj* are associated strictly with Makkah al-Mukarramah and its neighbouring places, Mina, Arafat, and Muzdalifa. *Hajj* cannot be performed in any month other than Zil-Hijjah, or on dates other than the prescribed ones for this purpose, or at places other than Makkah, Mina, Arafat, and Muzdalifa. The wisdom and objectives of *Hajj* necessitate that this great religious deed is performed in the same month, on the same dates, and at the same places. In fact, *Hajj* is a commemoration and imitation of the zeal of Prophet's Ibrahim and Ismail for *Tawheed* (Oneness of Allah) and their love for Allah and readiness to sacrifice the best and the dearest for His pleasure which were actually exhibited centuries ago at the same place and time. This noble emulation has a great power to create in believers' hearts love for Allah and ability to sacrifice their interests for Him. It also relieves them from subjugation to man-made laws, customs, and practices. Furthermore, the noble objective of keeping the Muslims throughout the world tied to the culture of Prophet Ibrahim, to Makkah as the centre of Islam, and to *Baitullah* (House of Allah) cannot ever be fulfilled without letting all Muslims perform *Hajj* at the same place and time.

III

ISLAMIC SOCIETY

FEATURES, FESTIVALS AND CUSTOMS

Prominent Features:
Islam a Religion of Ordained Divine Laws

The first prominent characteristic of Muslims all over the world is reflected in the fact that they follow a religion with prescribed tenets of faith and permanent and unchanging codes of laws. In fact, the term "religion" does not fully describe the true nature of Islam and is sometimes a cause of misunderstanding. The name of the followers of Islam, Muslims, is not related to a race, family, religious leader, founder of a religion, or country. It is related to a word which stands for a specific faith and way of life. The followers of other religions take their names from their religious leaders, prophets, countries, or races. Jews are called "Judaist" and "Children of Israel" (Bani Israel) after their religious leaders: "Judah" is the name of a son of Prophet Yaqoob (Jacob), and "Israel" is that of Prophet Yaqoob (Jacob) himself. Christians call themselves after Jesus Christ. Zoroastrians take their name from "Zorathust", the founder of that religion. Budhist call themselves after "Budha", the central figure in that religion. This is also true about many other religions of the world.

Title of the Muslim Ummah

But Muslims, who are referred to as *Muslimoon* and *Ummate Muslimah* in the Quran, other scriptures, and books of history and literature, are called so after the word *Islam*, which means "total submission (to Allah)". The religion thus named engenders in its adherents an outlook and attitude leading them to a lifestyle which is based on high and noble objectives. Muslims love Prophet Muhammad--blessings and peace be on him--very dearly, but in spite of this strong attachment they did not take the name *Muhammadan*. It were the British who wrongly used for the first time the term *Muhammadan* for Muslims. The Muslims who were aware of the true spirit of Islam objected to this misnomer and preferred for themselves the same old term, Muslim. Accordingly, the institutions in India which were named in the early days of the British rule as *Muhammadan*, later changed the term *Mohammadan* to *Muslim* in their names. [1]

Importance of Religion for Muslims

Religion occupies a pivotal position in the personal, social, and cultural lives of Muslims due to which they are extremely sensitive in matters relating to their faith. It is, therefore, pertinent that this important point is not overlooked whenever any problem relating to Muslims, individual or collective, moral or social, legal or constitutional, is taken into

[1]For example, when Anglo-Oriental Mohammadan College, Aligarh (India), was changed to a university, it was renamed as Muslim University. Similarly, the famous Mohammadan Educational Conference held at Aligarh in India was later referred to as Muslim Educational Conference.

consideration. That is why Muslims are so particular about the Islamic laws governing their affairs, which are popularly known as Muslim Personal Law. In fact, the fundamental part of the Muslim Personal Law is derived directly from the Quran itself whereas the details and explanations are based on Traditions and Islamic Jurisprudence.

The Muslim Personal Law is an integral part of the Islamic Shari'a (Islamic Code of Laws) and religion and is duly authenticated by the Quran and Hadith. It has not been developed independently by Muslim researchers, social scientists, lawyers or reformers. It, therefore, cannot be changed even by a Muslim government. It is a part of the religion of Islam because in Islam the jurisdiction of religion is not limited to faith and devotional services only; it also covers mutual relationships, rights and duties, and social values and customs. If culture and social life are separated from religion, religion becomes ineffective, and culture and social life become the agents of the wild desires and selfish interests of people.[2]

Islamic Laws (*Shari'a*) Unalterable

A part of Islamic Laws (*Shari'a*) is based so certainly on the verses of the Quran, or is authenticated by the continuous practice of Muslims, or has had full consensus of Muslim scholars that any Muslim rejecting it will be legally and in principle considered a renegade. Regardless of the difficulty in practising such Islamic Laws due to changes in time, they

[2]For further elucidation of this point, see the Author's book on the Muslim Personal Law.

cannot be altered. Even a popularly elected government of a Muslim country has no right and power to change such fundamental laws. If, in case, such an attempt is made, it will be illegal and will mean a direct interference in religion.

There is, however, another kind of Islamic laws which are developed on the basis of the Muslim scholars' understanding and interpretation of Islamic rulings and in which there is scope for a change. Such laws could be readjusted to meet the demands of the changing time by Muslim scholars and jurists who would do so after due discussions among themselves and thorough consideration of all implications involved. This process is allowed in Islam, has always been at work in all periods of Islamic history, and is necessary to be continued till the last generation of Muslims lives on earth.

Specific Concept of Purification (*Taharah*)

Another distinctive characteristic of the Muslim Ummah is their specific concept of purification (*Taharah*). This could be appreciated only when we understand how Muslims differentiate between cleanliness and purification. While cleanliness means a state in which the body and dress of a person are free of dirt, purification in Islam means that the body or dress of a person is not polluted by any unclean thing, such as urine, stool, wine, blood, dog's saliva, and excrement of an unclean bird. If even a drop of any of these falls on the body or clothes of a person, he will, Islamically speaking, be considered impure and thus unfit for offering prayers in that state, even if his body and dress look perfectly clean. In the same way if he has not washed his private parts after passing urine or stool, or if he needs a bath after having sexual intercourse or wet dream, he is impure and cannot offer prayers in that state. The same rule applies to utensils, floor, or earth. It is not necessary that if they are clean and spotless, they are also pure. In all such instances of impurity one has to purify himself, his dress or any other thing according to Islamic injunctions, after which he will be qualified again to offer prayers to his Lord and use his dress or any such thing in a regular way.

Eating Habits

Muslims are not free in eating and drinking as they like. A line of demarcation has been drawn for them in the Islamic *Shari'a* (Code of Law) between *Halal* (Permissible) and *Haram* (Prohibited) which they are not allowed to cross. They cannot use the meat of an animal or that of a bird unless they slaughter it Islamically and pronounce Allah's name over it. If an animal or a bird is not slaughtered Islamically, its meat is just like that of a dead animal or bird. Similarly, if an animal is slaughtered in the name of somebody other than Allah--may it be a goddess, a god, an idol, a prophet, a saint, or a martyr--it is also like a dead animal for Muslims which is prohibited for them to eat. The dog and the pig are considered unclean in Islam and are prohibited for Muslims. Some other animals-- lions, tigers, leopards and the like--are not considered unclean but Muslims are forbidden to eat their meat. Similarly, the meat of birds that use claws to eat or that of hunting birds is forbidden, whereas the meat of birds eating with their beaks is permissible. These rules of eating are, in fact, based on the model of the culture established by Prophet Ibrahim which Muslims are required to follow, no matter at what time or place in the human history they happen to live.

Love for the Prophet

Another distinctive characteristic of Muslims is their extraordinary but balanced love for their Prophet, blessings and peace be on him. He is not merely respected by Muslims as a messenger of Allah, an ideal person, and a great religious leader; he is also loved very dearly and very sincerely by them. But there is always a balance between their love for him and their love for Allah the Almighty.[3] They do not ascribe to the Prophet any attribute essentially characteristic of Allah and do not treat him with any kind of exaggerated veneration, as was done by the followers of some other prophets. It is related in a Hadith that the Prophet of Allah, blessings and peace be on him, asked his followers not to raise him higher than his limits and not to commit any excesses in his veneration, as the Christians did with their Prophet. He added that when he had to be mentioned, he should be mentioned as "Allah's slave and messenger".

It is, therefore, important to understand that in addition to faith in Prophet Muhammad's messengership, Muslims nourish truly unique and unprecedented love for him, may Allah's blessings and peace descend in abundance on him. It would not be an exaggeration at all to say that hundreds of thousands of Muslims love him more than themselves, their parents and children and consider it their first duty to protect the honour of his name against any desecration. They cannot ever tolerate any attempt to stigmatize his personality. They

[3]For details, see *Muhammad Rasoolullah* by the author (Lucknow: Academy of Islamic Research and Publications, 1979). The book is also available in Arabic, Urdu, and Hindi.

are so sensitive in this matter that they do not hesitate in even sacrificing their lives in such an inauspicious situation. Evidence testifying to it will easily be found in each period of time. Even today the Prophet's name, his city, his sayings, and anything else bearing a relationship with him are dearest to Muslims.

The sincerity with which the Muslims pray for the Prophet, the eagerness with which they invoke Allah's blessings on him, the large number in which his biographies are written in different languages of the world, and the rich poetic compositions in which the poets have paid tribute to him stand unmatched in the world history.

Faith in Cessation of Prophethood

Muslims also believe that Prophet Muhammad--blessings and peace be on him--is the last of the prophets of Allah with whom the divine system of prophethood and revelation came to an end forever. If anybody claims to be a prophet of Allah after him, he is a liar and an impostor. This belief is fully substantiated by the Quran and the Traditions and has been held by Muslims continuously from the Prophet's time to this day. In fact, this belief has always served the Muslims as a strong boundary line protecting them in all ages from falling a prey to shrewd contrivers.

Love for the Prophet's Comapanions and His Family

Muslims consider it necessary to respect and hold in high esteem the Companions of the Prophet called *Sahahah*--those who lived in the days of the Prophet and benefitted from his company. Muslims consider them as their ideal and feel grateful to them for their selfless scarifices and great contributions. Whenever they mention any of them, they say, "May Allah be pleased with them" after his name. Out of them four illustrious Companions--Abu Bakr, Umar, Uthman, and Ali--may Allah be pleased with all of them--who became the caliphs of the Muslims successively after the demise of the Prophet are considered the most repectable among the Prophet's Companions and their names are mentioned after the Prophet's in the sermons of the Friday and Eid Prayers. Muslims also show special respect to six more Companions to whom the Prophet, blessings and peace be on him, conveyed glad tidings of the grant of paradise by Allah in their very lifetime. These ten Companions are called "the Ten Recepients of the Glad Tiding" ('*Ashra Mubashshara*).

Muslims also hold dear the family members of the Prophet (called *Ahle Bait*) which include his wives, daughters, and grandsons (Imam Hasan and Imam Husain). Muslims always remember them with love and respect. They consider their love for the Prophet's family members as a natural outcome of their love for the Prophet.

Reverence for the Holy Quran

Muslims hold the Holy Quran in great reverence. They do not consider the Quran as merely a book of wise sayings, moral teachings, and social laws to be put into practice whenever convenient. They rather take it as a Word of Allah and a Divine Revelation from beginning to end both in word and meaning, which is fully secure from alteration. They touch it only when they are clean, read it after making ablution, and keep it respectfully at a high place.

Tradition of Committing the Quran to Memory

Throughout the world Muslims follow the practice of committing the Quran to memory. There are special learning centres established for this purpose where students are taught the formal science of pronunciation in Arabic (*Tajweed*) and where they learn the Quran by heart. In India alone, for instance, the number of *Huffaz* (persons who have memorized the whole Quran) has increased now to hundreds of thousands. Among them there are such *Huffaz* who could conveniently recite the whole Quran in one night (as they do in *Taraweeh* prayers in Ramadan). There are also such pious *Huffaz* who recite the complete Quran every day in the month of Ramadan. There are also children of ten to twelve years who learn by heart the whole Quran and can recite it with perfect ease.[4] In every age there has also been a good number of women *Huffaz* everywhere in the world.[5]

[4]To help non-Muslim readers understand the difficulty of the task it should be mentioned here that the Holy Quran contains three-hundred-forty thousand, seven hundred, and forty (340,740) words. The Quran printed in Egypt usually consists of 800 to 900 pages. In India it it usually printed in 600 to 800 pages.

[5]When I was a boy, there were about twelve women *Huffaz* in my small family itself, in which my mother, a maternal aunt, a paternal aunt, a maternal uncle's wife, and a maternal aunt's daughter were my close relatives. They used to lead women in *Taraweeh* prayers in Ramadan at home and recite the whole Quran in that month. A large number of women used to attend.

A Global Community

A very important characteristic of Muslims, which should be appreciated in its realistic context, is that Muslims consider themselves an international community and their religion an international religion joining coreligionists beyond the limitations of race, language, and nationality. They take interest in the common international Islamic problems, are influenced by the problems of Muslim nations, and extend sympathy and moral support to each other to the possible extent and within the provisions of the laws of their countries. They do not consider it against their love and faithfulness for their country of residence. They always have sincere love for their motherland and wish to contribute in the best possible way to its prosperity and progress. They consider their attachment for the Muslims living in other parts of the world as an outcome of their faith in religion, justice, and noble human nature and take it to be a source of benefit and stability for their country as well. The Indian Muslims have always been in the forefront in this regard. The enthusiasm with which they sided with the Turks in the famous Khilafat Movement, the zeal with which they formed Khilafat Committees, the sincerity due to which they won the support of the whole India and most notably that of the greatest leader of India Gandhiji, and the way in which the Khilafat leaders--the Ali brothers, Maulana Azad and Maulana Abdul Bari--raised up the whole country on this issue are events of the recent past. This is a distinctive characteristic of the Muslim community and a natural result of its educational and historical backgrounds. It is necessary to take into consideration this fact before any decision relating to Muslims is taken.

Important Festivals:

Eid al-Fitr and *Eid al-Adha*

There are two major festivals of Muslims: Eid al-Fitr and Eid al-Adha. Eid al-Fitr occurs immediately after the month of Ramadan, on the first day of the month of Shawwal which is the tenth month in the Islamic calendar. As Ramadan is the month of fasting, renunciation and self-discipline, Muslims, quite naturally, eagerly await sighting of the moon of Eid al-Fitr. On the twenty-ninth of Ramadan, Muslims of all ages and ranks eagerly try to sight the moon. If the moon is not sighted on the twenty-ninth, Muslims fast the following day and try to sight the moon on the thirtieth. When the moon is sighted, Muslims happily greet and congratulate each other. Youngers offer respectful greetings and salutations to elders. Children run to the elderly members of the family and women with the happy news of the sighting of the moon and are rewarded with good wishes and blessings. Those who are educated and wish to follow the tradition of the illustrious Prophet of Allah, blessings and peace be on him, recite the following prayer at the sight of the moon:

(O moon)! my
Sustainer as well as
Yours is Allah. You
are the moon of
guidance and
blessings. O Allah!
let this month begin
with us with peace

and belief, security
and obedience, and
guidance to the deeds
that please You.

Preparations for Eid al-Fitr

Preparations for Eid al-Fitr begin quite a few days in advance. Especially at night before the Eid day there is so much liveliness and excitement at home as well as in the market. Preparations for Eid begin quite early in the morning. To mark the ending of the month of fasting, Muslims take their breakfast in the morning and start preparing for the Eid prayer. They take a bath, wear new dress (if they could afford), apply perfume and proceed to the place where congregational prayer for Eid is be held. Before they go for prayer, they offer a charity in cash or grain to the poor, which is called *Sadaqatul Fitr*. This charity is, as a matter of fact, a gesture on the part of Muslims to express their thankfulness to the Lord for the blessings of fasting. It is offered to the poor by all financially well-off Muslim men and women for themselves as well as for their children including the infants. To offer the Eid al-Fitr prayer after the sunrise was the pratice of the illustrious Prophet, blessings and peace be on him. The earlier it is offered after the sunrise, the better.

Eid al-Fitr Prayer

When Muslims proceed for Eid al-Fitr prayer, they keep on proclaiming Allah's praise and their thankfulness to Him in a low voice. Following the practice of the Prophet of Allah, blessings and peace be on him, they prefer to go for prayer by one way and return by another so that Allah's glory may well be proclaimed and their attachment to religion as well as their unity may well be reflected.

For Eid prayer there is no *Iqamah* (final call marking the commencement of the prayer), nor are any *Sunnah* or *Nafl* prayers said before it. When Muslims gather and the time fixed for prayers arrives, the Imam advances and leads the prayer. After completing the prayer, he mounts to the pulpit and delivers the Eid al-Fitr sermon. This sermon usually sheds light on the true spirit and message of Eid al-Fitr, religious laws concerning it, and needs and demands of the current time.

Eid al-Adha:
Importance of Sacrifice in It

In Eid al-Adha an additional deed of sacrificing an animal in the name of Allah is performed. *Sadaqatul Fitr* (charity given in Eid al-Fitr) is not offered in Eid al-Adha. This festival falls on the 10th of Dhil Hijjah, the twelfth month in the Arabic calendar. This is the day when the pilgrims complete rituals of *Hajj* (Pilgrimage) and come to stay at a place called *Mina*, which is four miles from Makkah. The pilgrims then engage themselves as best as possible in remembering Allah, offering prayers, sacrificing animals. and enjoying with gratitude food and other gifts of Allah.

As against Eid al-Fitr which is celebrated for one day, Eid al-Adha continues for three days. The Eid al-Adha prayer is offered on the 10th of Dhil Hijjah, but sacrifices can be offered up to the 12th. In Eid al-Adha some special words marking

Allah's praise and glory are said loudly by worshippers after each obligatory prayer, beginning with *Salatal Fajr* (Morning Prayer) of the 9th of Dhil Hijjah and continuing upto the *Salatal 'Asr* (Afternoon Prayer) of the 13th. These are called *Takbirate Tashreeq* which are as follows:

Allah is the greatest,
Allah is the greatest.
None is worthy of
worship except Allah.
Allah is the greatest,
Allah is the greatest.
And all praise is
for Him.

The meat of the sacrificed animal is divided into three parts: one part for the family, the other for friends, and the third for the poor and needy. The three days of Eid al-Adha are marked as happy days for eating and drinking and Muslims are instructed not to fast on these days (or on the day of Eid al-Fitr). Usually Muslims eat good food in Eid al-Adha; even poor persons get to eat good food, such as meat, in abundance that day.

Global Dimension of Both Festivals

Eid al-Fitr and Eid al-Adha are international festivals of Muslims which are celebrated by them all over the world irrespective of their national, social, or financial differences. That is why in all countries of the world, whether Muslims live there in majority or in minority, these festivals are celebrated more or less in the same manner. Such a uniformity is possible only because the rituals followed in these festivals are determined by the Quran and the Hadith and have been observed uniformly since the days of the Prophet, blessings and peace be upon him.

Important Customs:

from Birth to Death

The Islamic Shari'a fully covers a Muslim's life from birth to death reminding him at every step that he is a bondsman of Allah, a member of the Ummah of the Prophet of Islam, and a follower of a specific way of life. He thus remembers that he should take the religious code of Islam as his guide and try to live by sincerely adhering to it until his last moment in this world.

Birth of a Child and Calling *Adhan* and *Iqamah* in His Ears

When a baby is born in a Muslim family, a pious person from the family or neighbourhood first calls *Adhan* (prayer call) in his right ear and *Iqamah* (call marking the beginning of the prayer) in his left. The *Adhan* and the *Iqamah* are specifically related to *Salah* (prayer) and the baby quite obviously does not understand the meaning and implication of such calls. The aim behind this pratice, however, is that the baby should first of all hear the name of Allah and call for His worship in this world. It is also a practice to put a very small piece of a date chewed by a pious person for this purpose in the mouth of the baby as a mark of blessing. This practice is authenticated by a tradition of the Prophet of Allah.

Shaving the Head of the Child

It is *Mustahab*[6] to shave the head of the child (called *Aqeeqah*) on the seventh day of his birth. If it is not done then, it could be done on the fourteenth, or even later. Two goats are sacrificed at the birth of a male child and one at that of a female one. The meat of the sacrificed animal is distributed among the poor and relatives. It is also cooked in the family and is eaten and fed to others. *Aqeeqah*, however, is not obligatory on Muslims nor is sacrificing of animals. If one is not financially well off to bear the expenses of sacrificing an animal, he does not have to do it.

Giving a Name to the Child

Usually on the occasion of *Aqeeqah* the child is given a name. A pious person from the family or neighbourhood suggests the name, or the parents themselves select a name of their choice. Arabic names belonging to Islamic traditions are preferred so that the religious affiliation of the child may be reflected from his name. Muslim thinkers believe that there are definite psychological benefits of this pratice. The Islamic Shari'a has not made Muslims responsible for any specific names. It has, however, provided guidance that the best names for Muslims are those which reflect man's bondsmanship to Allah alone (which is the essence of *Tawheed*, belief in the Oneness of God). That is why most Muslim names begin with the word "'Abd" (slave), such as 'Abdullah, 'Abdur Rahman, 'Abdul Wahid, 'Abdul 'Ahad, 'Abdus Samad, 'Abdul 'Azeez,

---

[6] An act which fetches rewards if done, but, if missed, is not punishable.

and 'Abdul Majeed.[7] It has also been emphazised that a Muslim name should not contain any word suggesting arrogance and disobedience. Accordingly, names such as *Malikul Mulk* (ruler of the universe) and *Shahanshah* (King of Kings) are disapproved.

Adopting Names of Prophets and *Sahabah*[8]

In selecting a name for a child, a Muslim's mind is first directed toward the name of the Prophet of Allah and those of his Companions and other Prophets. A Muslim gives one of these names to his child as a mark of good wishes hoping that it would attract Allah's mercy.

It is interesting to note that although Prophet Muhammad is a descendant of Prophet Isma'il and that the Jews are descendents of Prophet Ishaque, Muslims frequently take names of the Prophets from the descendents of Prophet Ishaque (known as *Bani Israil*) in spite of long-standing differences between the Muslims and the Jews. This is so because according to the teachings of Islam all Prophets are to be respected and believed in, whether they are from *Bani Israel* (Children of Israil) or *Bani Isma'il* (Children of Isma'il). Muslims do not have any prejudice in choosing names for themselves. That is why in India alone, for example, millions of Muslims are named after Prophet Ishaq and his children. They are thus called, *Ishaque, Yaqoob, Yusuf, Dawood,*

---

[7]The second parts of these names are names of Allah signifying His attributes.

[8]Companions of Prophet Muhammad, blessings and peace be on him.

Sulaiman, Musa, Haroon, Isa, Imran, Zakariya, and *Yahiya*--
all of whom are from the *Bani Israil* tribe. Likewise, in
Muslim women *Maryam, Safura,* and *Asiya* are common
names, which are the names of pious women form the *Bani
Israil* clan.

Teaching the Child Etiquette of Purification

When the child attains an age of general understanding and
responsibility, he is taught to keep himself clean and
unpolluted. He is instructed to wash with water after passing
urine or stool and protect his body and clothes from getting
unclean and polluted.

Teaching the Child How to Pray

At this stage the child is taught how to perform ablution
(*Wudu*) and is encouraged to say prayers. The father or any
other elderly member of the family often takes him to the
mosque where he joins congregational prayers with others. It is
related in a Tradition of the Prophet of Allah, blessings and
peace be on him, that when a child reaches the age of seven, he
should be asked to perform his prayer, and when he is ten he
should be strictly instructed in this matter and punished if he
ignores.

Teaching the Child Islamic Manners

At this age, parents, especially educated Muslims, teach
children Islamic manners. For example, children are taught
that good things (such as eating, drinking, shaking hands)
should be done with the right hand and other acts (such as

cleaning after natural calls) with the left. They are also taught that they should drink water in a sitting posture and, if possible, in three breaths, that elders should be respectfully greeted, that *Alhamdulillah* ("All Praise is for Allah") should be said after sneezing, *Bismillah* ("To begin with the name of Allah") in the beginning of eating food, and words of thankfulness at the end. Muslims also teach their children at this age short chapters from the Quran as well as supplications and words for Allah's glorification to be said on different occasions. Children are also told then stories about prophets and other pious persons so that they take such people as their ideal and learn to live virtuously.

When the child attains adulthood, *Salah* (Prayers), *Sawm* (Fasting) and, if necessary conditions apply, *Zakah* (Poor-Due) and *Hajj* (Pilgrimage) become obligatory (*Fard*) on him. If he does not observe them, he commits a sin. Now, the rules of *Halal* (Permissible) and *Haram* (Forbidden), reward and punishment apply to him and he becomes responsible for his deeds in this world and in the hereafter.

Marriage

In Islam rites of marriage are very easy and brief. Marriage is a solemn pledge legalizing union between a man and a woman and is regarded in Islam a good deed deserving reward. Only the two words of agreement and acceptance and two witnesses are needed for the performance of marriage. Islam wants to ensure that such a relationship between man and woman is not established in an irresponsible way. That is why marriage is announced and made public by involving two persons from the society as witnesses. The male partner should consider it necessary to pay to his wife a marriage gift (*Mehr*) and take the responsibility of protecting her honour and providing her with necessities of life according to his standard of living. Nothing else is needed for marriage.

The early Muslims performed marriage in a very simple way. A glaring example of it is the marriage of Abdur Rahman bin Awf, a Companion of the Prophet. He had emigrated from Makkah in love of the Prophet and had a very close relationship with him, but he did not invite even the Prophet to his marriage, although the Prophet's presence on the occasion would have been a source of blessing and a matter of honour for him. In spite of the fact that the Muslim community in Madinah al-Munawwara was small and closely knit, the Prophet did not even know about this marriage. He learnt about it later. More importantly, he did not complain that he was not informed.

How a Muslim Marriage Is Performed

It is closer to the *Sunnah* (Tradition of the Prophet) that the father or a *Wali*[9] of the bride should give her in marriage because the Prophet, blessings and peace be on him, had himself given his daughter Fatima in marriage to Ali. At this time two witnesses and a *Wakeel*[10] go to the bride to obtain her

---

[9] In Islamic Jurisprudence, a *Wali* is a male relative of the bride who is adult and mentally sound and who is entitled by the Islamic Code of Law to act in such matters.

[10] A *Wakeel* is an authorized representative of a person by his consent or order to conduct his affairs on his behalf.

consent for her marriage with the groom. Generally, the witnesses and the *Wakeel* are members of the family and relatives of the bride. Then the man who is responsible for performing the marriage delivers a brief sermon which consists of verses of the Quran, relevant sayings of the Prophet, and supplications, all in the Arabic language. He then asks the groom to pronounce his acceptance of his marriage with the girl. The groom gives his acceptance of the marriage in an audible voice and clear terms. He also offers or promises to offer to the bride a sum of money called *Mehr*[11] in Islamic terminology. With this the marriage is complete. Then all present in the gathering lift their hands to Allah in supplication and pray for the couple to remain united in love and affection and lead a happy conjugal life.

The Marriage Sermon

The marriage sermon covers mutual rights and responsibilities of marriage partners. Generally, it is given in Arabic. Recently, some scholars in India and Pakistan have adopted the practice of delivering a brief sermon in Urdu after the Arabic sermon to project the true spirit of marriage and responsibilities involved in the language that the people present understand. Thus, instead of becoming an entertainment party, the marriage gathering is used to inform

---

[11] "*Mehr* is a marriage gift offered by the groom to the bride as a token of love, good will and future financial support. It is a way to assure the bride that the groom wishes to share with her his life, love, and resources. In Islam it is forbidden for the groom to demand any dowry from the family of the bride directly or in an implied way. It is he who pays *Mehr* to the bride.

and instruct the bridegroom and guests about the noble spirit and values of marriage that Islam attempts to inculcate in its followers.

A Model Marriage Sermon

Below is given the text of a sermon which was delivered a few years ago on the occasion of a marriage and which reflects the essential mood and spirit of marriage in Islam. It is reproduced from a tape.

"O mankind! reverence your
Guardian-Lord, Who created
you from a single person,
created, of like nature,
his mate, and from them twain
scattered (like seeds) countless
men and women; reverence God
through Whom ye demand
your mutual (rights), and
(reverence) the wombs
(that bore you): for God
ever watches over you. "
    [IV : 1]

"O ye who believe! fear
God as He should be
feared, and die not
except in a state of Islam. "
    [III : 102]

100

"O ye who believe! fear
God, and (always) say
a word directed to the right,
that He may make your
conduct whole and sound
and forgive you your sins:
he that obeys God and
His Apostle, has already
attained the highest
achievement."
[XXXIII : 70-71]

"Gentlemen! in Islam marriage is not only an observance of a custom or a fulfillment of a desire of the self. Observed with correct intention, this practice is an act of worship, nay, a combination of several acts of worship. It does not involve only one religious law; several religious laws are related to it. It has a place in the Quran and in the Hadith and is discussed in detail in a separate section in books of Islamic jurisprudence. But unfortunately its true spirit is ignored by careless Muslims more than that of any other *Sunnah* (a deed established by the Prophet's practice). Rather, the occasion of marriage is used now-a-days for disobeying Allah, obeying the Satan, gratifying the desires of the self, and adhering to un-Islamic rites and customs.

"The institution of marriage bears a complete message for our lives which is so very well reflected in the verses of the Quran read by the Prophet of Allah, blessings and peace be on him, on the occasion of a marriage and which I recited in the beginning of my address. In the first verse there is a mention of the genesis of the human race which is indeed very appropriate

101

for this occasion and may be taken here as a good omen as well. In the beginning Prophet Adam was alone in the world but when Allah joined him with his life partner Eve, the human race multiplied and now the whole world is filled with their progeny. Surely, then, it is not at all difficult for Allah to increase in number the two persons who are getting married today in His name.

"Allah the Almighty says further in the same verse: 'Reverence through Whom ye demand your mutual (rights).' Gentlemen! the whole life is covered with the episodes of seeking of help and granting of it. Trade, government, and education, for example, are all inspired by a spirit of goodwill in which one party solicits and the other gratifies. This is a characteristic of civilized life. What is marriage? It is also a civilized way to solicit a person's consent for joining the other as life partner.

"The family of the groom ask another family for a bride for their son suggesting that his life will be completed only through that union. The other family give their happy acceptance. Then the two persons are united in marriage in the name of Allah. Thus, they who may have been totally unknown to each other join each other in trust and intimacy which is inconceivable in any other relationship. The fate of one thus gets united to that of the other and their happiness and gratification become interdependent. This is, indeed, the miracle of Allah's name which through marriage transforms a forbidden relationship to a legal act and turns an otherwise sinful act into a rewarding deed. Thus marriage revolutionizes the lives of the two persons.

"After that Allah the Almighty reminds people to remain mindful of the sanctity of His name on the basis of which they enter into marriage with each other. It would be shameful if one selfishly exploits the rights gained through marriage but ignores the duties involved. Allah also mentions here that the couple entering into marriage should also remain mindful of the rights of their relatives ("and reverence the wombs that bore you"). There is a need that on the occasion of the establishment of a new relationship the importance of previous relationships is emphasized. The new relationship does not nullify the previous relationships. It should not happen that a man remembers the rights of his wife and ignores those of his mother; or that he discards his father in an effort to serve his father-in-law. If a person thinks that his transgressions in this regard would go unnoticed, he should know that Allah is watching him all the time ("for God ever watches over you"). Allah is indeed such a witness Who is with him all the time, closer to him than even his jugular veins.

"In the next verse a bitter but unavoidable reality, the death, is mentioned. In fact, it requires the courage of a prophet to mention death on a happy occasion such as that of a marriage so that man does not forget his ultimate end and prepares well to depart from the world in the best state of *Iman* (Faith). The mention of death here implies that no matter how happy and prosperous one's life may be, one should make sincere efforts that he breathes his last in the state of faith and meets his Lord as one truly faithful to Him.

The third verse of the Quran recited earlier commands the believers to fear Allah and always say what is true and right. It is as if the groom is being reminded here that by saying the

103

words, "I accept" he makes a serious covenant and takes upon himself a great responsibility. It is further stated that if a person learns to conduct himself in a responsible manner all the time, his whole life, sayings and doings will reflect truth and honesty making him an ideal figure deserving Allah's forgiveness and pleasure. The Quranic verse concludes with the reminder that the real success of a person lies in his obedience to Allah and the Prophet, not in the gratification of the self or adherence to false traditions."[12]

To distribute dates on the occasion is an act of *Sunnah* (Prophetic tradition).

Marriage a Form of Worship

In Islam marriage is not regarded as merely a fulfillment of a natural human need; it is considered an act of worship which, if performed with an understanding of higher religious and spiritual values involved, wins to a person a state of closeness to Allah. The Prophet of Allah, blessings and peace be on him, set a practical example of the noblest possible married life. He also said, "He is the best among you who is the best for his family, and I am the best for my family". The respect for women engendering sincere consideration for their emotion and sensitivity that was Prophet Muhammad's natural disposition is not found in the practical lives of even the acclaimed champions of women's cause or famous spiritual leaders and saints; in fact, it is difficult to find it even in the lives of other Prophets, blessings and peace be on them. Prophet Muhammad's respectful treatment of his pious wives,

[12]The marriage sermon ends here.

participation in their recreations (which were Islamically permissible), thoughtfulness for their emotions, and justice in dealing with them are qualities that remain unparallel.

Even with children the Prophet of Allah, blessings and peace be on him, was so considerate that he cut short his prayers (*Salah*) if a child of a woman praying behind him started crying during the prayers. This was the highest level of sacrifice on his part as no other act was dearer to him than performing prayers.

Natural Problems and a Muslim's Response

Now we will deal with some natural, day-to-day problems that occur in a Muslim's life and the characteristic way in which a Muslim responds to them.

Illness

Illness is a part of life, but a Muslim is not excused from performing his regular prayers even when he is ill. He, nevertheless, is granted various concessions in the state of sickness. For example, if he is unable to go to the mosque, he can say his prayers at home. If he cannot stand up for prayers, he is allowed to pray in a sitting posture. If it is difficult for him to sit, he can say prayers lying in bed. If even that is difficult, he should say his prayers just by gestures. If using water for ablution is harmful for his health, he can say his prayers by performing *Tayammum*.[13]

To visit a sick person is considered an act deserving great reward in Islam. The visitor, however, is instructed not to stay long with a sick person, as it could cause inconvenience to him. If the sick person needs company, the visitor can surely stay with him as long as needed.

Death

In man's life ultimately comes the inevitable stage of death which spares none, whatever his religion, nationality, or race. We will present here a brief account of the specific attitude, rites and practices with which Muslims deal with this situation.

Concern for Meeting Death in a State of *Iman* (Faith)

A Muslim (even if he has not been a strong adherent to Islamic practices) is very much concerned for meeting death in a good state of *Iman*, i.e., he wants to leave this world by sincerely affirming his faith in the Oneness of Allah and in Prophet Muhammad as His true and last Prophet. It is a common tradition among Muslims that they request one another to pray for a death marked with Allah's favour. Even a common Muslim considers this as the greatest mark of success

---

[13]In *Tayammum* clean soil is used in a specific way to attain purification. It is allowed only when water for *Wudhu* is not available or is harmful for the health of the person concerned.

106

and truly envies the person who breathes his last with the name of Allah on his tongue.

When a Muslim reaches the last stage and is about to depart from the world, his relatives and friends instruct and encourage him to recite the words of the Islamic Faith ("There is no god but Allah and Muhammad is a Prophet of Allah"), or just the name of Allah. If he is unable to move his tongue, the people present on the scene themselves start reciting the above words or the name of Allah for him. If his tongue is dried, the holy *Zamzam* water or any other juice is dropped in his mouth. Then the person present start reciting the Quranic chapter *Yaseen* to invoke Allah's blessings for him. When his last moment comes, his face is turned toward the *K'aba* in the holy city of Makkah (the direction which he faced all his life in his prayers).

After the death of a person, preparations for giving him a final bath and shroud (*Kafan*) begin. For shroud new white cloth is used. For men it consists of an unstitched long shirt, a long piece of cloth for the lower part of the body, and a long sheet to cover the body from above. For women a piece of cloth to tie her hair and a second short shirt to wear inside the long shirt are added. The bath to the dead body is given in a certain way (ensuring respectfulness to the dead and full cleanliness to the body). Anybody can wash a dead body, but a person knowledgeable in the procedures followed in this matter is certainly preferred. Relatives and friends eagerly try to participate in doing this last service to the dead and consider it a duty apt to fetch great reward.

Congregational Prayer for the Dead

When the dead body is ready, properly washed and enshrouded, it is taken out for the final congregational prayer (*Salatul Janaza*). It is a highly rewarding act in Islam to participate in it. This prayer is congregational, but there is no kneeling (*Ruku'*) or prostration (*Sujood*) in it. People form rows, preferably in odd numbers, for the prayer to start. Then a religious scholar or any other pious person steps ahead, stands in front of the deadbody (facing his chest) and leads the prayer. Besides saying other recitations and supplications, the Muslims attending the prayer inaudibly say the following supplication:

O Allah! forgive from
us the living and the dead,
the present and the absent,
the male and the female.

O Allah! whomever You keep
alive, keep him alive on
Islam, and whomever You
want to die, let him
die with Faith (Iman).

If the deadbody is of a minor boy or girl, a second supplication is also said, which is as follows:

O Allah! make this child
my forerunner (one who goes
toward You ahead of me)

108

and my reward and provision
in store with You, and
one interceding for me on
the Day of Judgement and
accept his intercession for me.

Carrying the Deadbody to the Cemetery

After the prayer is finished, people carry the bier on their shoulders to the cemetery. In Islam, shouldering a bier, carrying it to the cemetery, and staying there until the burial are considered as deeds met with great rewards. So Muslims in general eagerly try to shoulder the bier which is thus taken to the cemetery even if the distance is long and the season rough. Now-a-days in large cities where cemeteries are often far away in the outskirts the bier is taken for burial in a large car or a van. However, leaving an exception for an uncontrollable situation and distance of the cemetery, carrying the bier on shoulders to the cemetery is an Islamic tradition established by the Prophet of Allah, blessings and peace be on him.

Burial Rites

The grave is kept ready before the arrival of the deadbody at the cemetery. When the deadbody arrives, a few persons get down into the grave and, with the help of others, carefully take the deadbody to the grave and place it there by turning its face toward the direction of K'aba (which all Muslims face when offering prayers). Then wooden planks are used to cover the grave above which soil is spread. People participate in putting soil over the grave. At that time the following verse of the Quran is on their tongue:

From the (earth) did
We create you, and
into it shall We
return you, and
from it shall We
bring you out once
again.
    [XX : 55]

When enough soil is put over the grave and it is given the shape of a grave, the relatives and friends of the deceased stay there further for a short while and pray for the deliverance of the deceased. They recite some portions of the Quran on the occasion, which is a *Sunnah* (a practice of the Prophet).

Sending Food to the Family of the Deceased

When a person dies in a family, usually the relatives and friends of the family send food for them. This custom is based on the understanding that the family of the deceased may not find it convenient to cook and should, therefore, be relieved of this task. This is, in fact, a *Sunnah* (a practice of the Prophet) intended to share the grief of the family of the deceased, which is still followed in the Muslim society. Food is sent for three times or three days, depending on the status of the deceased.

IV

ISLAMIC CULTURE

The Prophets of Allah do not only call people to the religion of Islam by presenting tenets of the Islamic Faith and its codes of law; they also pioneer a new culture, a new civilization, and a new way of life. Such a culture can aptly be called "Ibrahimi Culture". This culture has certain fundamental principles and characteristics which distinguish it from other cultures based on ignorance. This distinction may be seen in its spirit and principles as well as in its outward manifestations and details.

The first distinctive characteristic of the Islamic culture is the authentic religious beliefs, social ethics, and moral values on which it is based. This factor is commonly shared by Muslims all over the world, irrespective of their nationality, language, and dressing style. Due to this common feature Muslims from different parts of the world look like members of a family, easily identifiable as representatives of the same culture. Thus, the Muslims of the world have a specific culture of their own which could be best called the "Ibrahimi Culture".

The Ibrahimi Culture and Its Pioneers

Prophet Ibrahim, may Allah's blessings and peace be on him, was the founder of that God-worshipping culture which was based on the noble principle s of faith in the Oneness of

Allah, God-remembrance, truth, piety, mercy and virtue. His moral integrity and distinctive lifestyle, which are described in the following verses of the Quran, run into the veins of this culture.

For Abraham was,
without doubt, forebearing
(of faults), compassionate,
and given to look
to God.
    [XI : 75]

For Abraham was
most tender-hearted,
forebearing.
    [IX : 114]

Prophet Muhammad, who was from the progeny of Prophet Ibrahim and the last in the line of the Prophets, blessings and peace be on all of them, gave a new lease of life to this culture in his time. He brought it to completeness and perfection and promoted it to the position of an eternal and universal culture.

Three Features of the Ibrahimi Culture

The Ibrahimi Culture has three distinctive features: faith in the Being of Allah and its constant awareness, faith in the Oneness of Allah (as taught by the Prophets and laid down in the Quran), and belief in the nobility of mankind and their inherent right to equality and justice. To my best knowledge, these characteristics, which inspire the true spirit of the

Ibrahimi Culture, are not found with such a clear projection in any other culture.

First Feature:
Faith in the Being of Allah

Faith in the Being of Allah with constant awareness of it (keeping it in view all the time and following it in practice) is a distinctive feature of the Muslim culture and is an integral part of it. If we consider different Muslim cultures and civilizations as dresses of different fashions (affected by diverse tastes of different people, local considerations, seasonal variations, and outside influences), we find all the dresses deeply drenched in one colour (Faith in Allah) which reaches every fibre and thread. The frequent remembrance and mention of the name of Allah flow in the veins of the Muslim culture like life-giving blood.

When a baby is born in a Muslim family, *Adhan* (Islamic prayer call) is called as first words in his ears, making thus the baby hear and learn the name of Allah even before his own name. When he is seven days old, his *Aqeeqah* (shaving off the head) is performed and an Islamic name is given to him. Such names are preferred which reflect man's bondsmanship to Allah and Allah's Oneness. Babies are sometimes also given the names of the Prophets, who were the greatest monotheists of their times. When the child begins his schooling, he is first of all taught the name of Allah and verses of the Quran. At the time of marriage a Muslim man and a woman are united as wife and husband in the name of Allah and are made responsible to honour the sanctity of Allah's name for the rest of their lives. In the festival of Eid al-Fitr Muslims proclaim the name of Allah in the prescribed way and offer two *Rak'ahs* of Prayer of thankfulness. In Eid al-Adha animals are sacrificed in the name of Allah.

When a Muslim is in his death bed, he is encouraged by his relatives to utter the name of Allah as his last word in the world to ensure for him a noble death. When the news of the death of a Muslim reaches other Muslims, they automatically respond by saying: "To God we belong and to Him is our return" [II : 156].

During the burial rites the name of Allah is very frequently mentioned from the beginning to the end. Muslims say prayers for the forgiveness of the deceased as well as for themselves. invoking Allah's help for living in faithfulness to Him and departing from the world with true faith in Him. Then the dead person is laid into the grave, all present uttering the name of Allah. In the grave his face is turned toward the K'aba, the direction he faced in prayers all his life. After his burial, whenever a Muslim passes by his grave, he says prayers for his forgiveness and invokes Allah's blessings on him. Thus, the name of Allah accompanies a Muslim in his life's journey at every step from birth to death.

Those mentioned above are clearly important stages in life, but even in ordinary engagements of the daily life a Muslim remembers his Lord and mentions His name so frequently. He begins eating with the name of Allah and ends with words of thankfulness to Him. Those eager to follow the Sunnah (practices of the Prophet of Allah) eat and drink, put off and put on dress, enter and come out of the lavatory, in fact, do everything with the name of Allah on their tongues and His remembrance in their minds and hearts. When a Muslim sneezes, for example, he is instructed to say Allah's praise; the Muslim who hears him sneezing is required to invoke a prayer for him. Other parts of a Muslim's time are also full of Allah's remembrance. Expressions such as *Masha Allah* ("May Allah increase it"), *Insha Allah* ("If Allah wills so") and *La hawla wala quwwata illa billah* ("There is no power or strength except that which comes from Allah"), which are words taught by the Prophet to Muslims to remember Allah, have now become an essential part of the languages spoken by Muslims throughout the world. These are Muslims' characteristic ways to remember Allah and to remind others of Him. The culture, language, literature, and lifestyle of no other people are so profoundly influenced by faith in Allah's Being and constant awareness of it as are the culture, language, literature and lifestyl: of Muslims. This is the first universal feature of the Islamic culture.

Second Feature:
Faith in the Oneness of Allah

The second universal feature of the Islamic culture is Muslims' faith in the Oneness of Allah which is so strongly reflected in their lives, ranging from faith to practice, from worship to celebration. It is proclaimed five times from the minarets of their mosques that there is none deserving worship except Allah. It is required that their houses too remain free from decorations bearing polytheistic signs and symbols. Pictures, statues, and idols are forbidden in their religion to the extent that these have to be avoided even in the toys played by Muslim children. Whether it is a religious ceremony or a national festival, a birthday celebration of a religious or political leader or an occasion o f national flag hoistation--it is forbidden for Muslims to bow in front of idols and statues, stand in front of them in reverence with folded hands, and put flower wreaths around them. All such acts are contrary to their monotheistic culture. Wherever Muslims are adhering to the Islamic culture, they discard all such polytheistic practices. Any act defying Allah's Oneness in any form--in giving name to a baby, in taking an oath, in revering pious persons and saints, or the like--is against the teaching of Islam.

Third Feature:
Belief in the Nobility of Man

The third universal feature of the Islamic culture is belief in the nobility of man and in the fact that all human beings are essentially equal on humanitarian terms. This teaching is so strongly emphasized in Islam that a belief in it becomes a second nture of a Muslim and fully controls his mind and heart. Consequently, the practice of observing discrimination in the name of cast and the tradition of untouchability are totally alien to Muslims. A Muslim would take meals with any other Muslim, nay any human being, without hesitation. Persons, several in number and different in background, eat together from one plate, eat each other's left-over food and drink left-over water. The king and the slave stand together shoulder to shoulder with each other in prayers. A person with lesser social status but greater knowledge is entitled to lead the prayers, the most important responsibility in Islam, while the rich and the elite have to follow him by standing behind him.

Professions Neither Humble Nor Unchangeable in Islam

In the Islamic culture professions are not permanent in the sense that people cannot change them. Professions do not serve as a basis for dividing people into high and low categories in status. Muslims adopt a profession according to their need and convenience. Sometimes a profession is taken by only one person in a family, but in other instances a whole family may adopt a profession and continue with it for generations. This, however, has no religious significance in Islam. Whenever needed, a Muslim can quit his present profession and take a new one, to which there is no religious or social restriction.

Also, no profession is looked down upon in an Islamic society. In the holy cities of Makkah and Madinah in Saudi Arabia and in other Arab countries some very distinguished and respectable Muslim scholars and persons enjoying high social status use with their names titles signifying professions that their predecessors adopted, but which they themselves do not practice.[1] They do not feel ashamed of such titles nor do others consider them as persons coming from humble social background.

For example, Osama, a present Imam of the Holy al-Haram (the Grand Mosque in Makkah which is the most prestigious Islamic place of worship in the world) uses the family title *Khaiyat* (tailor). His late father Abdullah who also was an Imam of the Holy al-Haram at Makkah kept the family title *Khaiyat* as part of his name. Several other prominent scholars and dignitaries take as their surnames titles such as *Hallaq* (barber), *Zaiyat* (oilman), *Sawwaf* (cotten dealer), and *Qassab* (butcher).

117

Widow Marriage

In Islam a widow's second marriage is not considered a base and objectionable act. Islamic teachings and traditions extend full legal and moral support to it. This was a practice of the Prophet of Islam, blessings and peace be on him, and subsequently in every age and time distinguished Muslim scholars, revered spiritual leaders, and prestigious emperors took widows as their wives without hesitation and gave their widow sisters and daughters in marriage to others. This practice is widely observed by Muslims everywhere in the world and is considered a natural response to a practical situation in life.

Tradition of Greeting

Muslims exchange greetings at the time of meeting and departing for which they use same words everywhere in the world, irrespective of their national, cultural, and linguistic differences. The first person extends greetings by saying, *Assalamo 'alaikum* ("Peace be on you"), to which the other replies, *Wa 'alaikumus salam* ("Peace be on you, too").

Importance of Knowledge

The first revelation that came to Prophet Muhammad, blessings and peace be on him, in the Cave of Hira near Makkah in Saudi Arabia has thus been recorded in the Quran:

Read!
in the name of thy
Lord and Cherisher,
Who created --
created man, out of
a (mere) clot of
congealed blood:
Read! and thy
Lord is Most Bountiful, --
He Who taught (the use of)
the Pen, -- taught man
that which he knew
not.
     [XCVI : 1-5]

The Creator of the universe mentions this fact in this first revelation that the fate of knowledge is tied up with the pen. The Prophet who received this revelation in the seclusion of the Cave of Hira was unlettered and did not know how to use a pen. This is an unprecedented incident in the history of the world that the first revelation which comes down to an unlettered Prophet living among an unlettered people in a country where even knowledge of alphabets was not common begins with the word *Iqra* ("Read"). The unlettered Prophet is asked in this revelation "to read" which clearly signifies that his followers would not merely be receivers of knowledge; they would also advance knowledge and spread it. The age of this Prophet, thus, was not going to be an age of ignorance and antagonism to knowledge; it was to be an age of knowledge, reason, wisdom and true advancement.

There was a serious flaw in the thinking of the people at that time: the inherent relationship between knowledge and the Creator was lost as a result of which knowledge had digressed from its correct course. This lost relationship was reestablished by this revelation by emphasizing in it that knowledge, which was granted such a high position in the above verse, must begin with the name of Allah ("Read! in the name of thy Lord and Cherisher"). As knowledge was a gift of Allah to mankind, it could advance in a balanced way only under His guidance. This was a most revolutionary call given to the world which could not have been imagined by people at that time. If the intellectuals and literary masters of the world were invited to make a guess how the first revelation of Islam would begin, none who knew the nature and intellectual background of the unlettered nation destined to be its first recipient would have thought that it would begin with the word *Iqra* ("Read"). By mentioning "pen" in the first revelation of Islam, Allah the Almighty granted an exceedingly honourable position to knowledge although a pen was perhaps a truly rare thing to be found in a house of Makkah then.

It was, indeed, a revolutionary call proclaimed in the first revelation in Islam that the journey of knowledge should be undertaken and covered in the light of the injunctions of Allah, the Wise, the All-Knowing, because this journey was very ong, very arduous, very risky. This was a journey, symbolically speaking, in which caravans were plundered in broad daylight, the path ran through dangerous valleys and deep seas, and the travellers encountered harmful snakes and scorpions at each step. In this journey one surely needed not knowledge, but Allah as guide. If knowledge was allowed to

120

drift away from its purposeful course set by Allah, man would get involved and take pride in petty things such as creating ornate designs or amusing pastimes, or in harmful acts such as forcing two nations into armed clash, or in selfish pursuits such as finding ways to fill the ever-hungry stomach.

The first revelation in Islam quoted above also presents the eternal fact that there is no limit to knowledge ("[the Lord] taught man that which he knew not."). The present advancement of knowledge is a clear exposition of this truth. The scientific and technological knowledge which has enabled the modern man to land on the moon, fly in the space, and reduce the distance are achievements which could be best understood by pondering on the above verse.

Attitude Towards Fine Arts

Another feature of the Islamic culture is that it maintains a moderate, realistic, and careful attitude towards fine arts. It is fully appreciative of beauty, delicacy, tenderness and fineness, but it does reject some branches currently associated with fine arts in the West, such as dancing, painting of living beings, and carving of statues. In other areas, such as singing, it holds a moderate and careful position and allows them under necessary restrictions. In any case, excessive involvement in fine arts is against the purposeful lifestyle of a Muslim as it would tend to deprive him of piety, concern for the hereafter, and morality-- qualities which he is expected to nourish in himself.

Religion as Guardian of Life

Time is a proportionate and balanced mixture of stability and change, stagnation and movement. If it loses either of these characteristics, it will lose its relevance. Islam as a religion accepts this fact and is ready to make necessary accommodations, but it holds the position that as religion it has to guide life, not simply follow it. Religion, as Islam pleads, does not have to passively approve all changes. It is not lifeless like the needle of a barometer which moves up or down mechanically to measure the pressure of the atmosphere, or a weather-cock fixed on the top of a building which moves to show the direction of the wind. The function of religion is not simply to acknowledge and show the changes which are occurring at a time. Its obligation is to check whether a change is healthy or unhealthy, constructive or destructive. It has to evaluate the effect of a change on mankind at large and on its promoters in particular. It judges all pros and cons of a change before it approves it. It, therefore, will discourage a change if it is destructive. It may even oppose the latter kind.

At this point we can see a clear difference between religion and morality. Religion feels obliged to oppose wrong inclinations, whereas morality simply identifies them.

IV

ISLAMIC MORALITY

Refining Morals and Disciplining Self:
Objectives of Prophet Muhammad's Mission

Allah the Almighty has mentioned the fundamental aims and advantages of the mission of Prophet Muhammad, blessings and peace be on him, in several verses of the Quran. At one place it is mentioned:

A similar (favour have
ye already received)
in that We have sent
among you an Apostle
of your own, rehearsing to
you our signs, and
sanctifying you, and
instructing you in scripture
and wisdom and in
new knowledge.
    [II : 151]

In the missionary scheme of Prophet Muhammad, blessings and peace be on him, refining of morals and disciplining of the self occupy a very prominent place, as they do in the teachings of the Quran. The style and diction of the Quran suggest that by the word *Hikmah* (Wisdom) used in the above verse is meant high morals and Islamic etiquette. In the Chapter *Isra* in the Quran the fundamentals, principles and etiquette of morality are first discussed, and then morality and etiquette are referred to as *Hikmah* (Wisdom).

These are among the
(precepts of) wisdom,
which thy Lord has
revealed to thee.
[XXVII : 39]

The Prophet, blessings and peace be on him, himself stated the objective of his mission in these words:

I was raised but
for complementing
high morality.

He indeed was the best specimen and perfect example of the highest moral values, to which the Quran attests in these words:

And thou (standest)
on an exalted standard
of character.
[LXVIII : 4]

Also, when Aisha the Truthful, may Allah be pleased with her, was asked about the moral conduct of the Prophet, she put it in these words:

His conduct was
modelled on the
Quran.

The wisdom and refinement of the character of the Prophet permeated through the lives of his illustrious Companions. Under his care and company such a generation of his Companions was raised which developed the best moral qualities, discarded immoral and ignoble habits and inclinations, and overcame evils of ego, influence of ignorance and instigations of the devil. The words of the Prophet, blessings and peace be on him, bear witness to this fact:

The best people
are the people
of my age.
[Bukhari]

Abdullah bin Mas'ud, may Allah be pleased with him, has described the excellence of the Companions of the Prophet in the following words which are comprehensive and compact:

Pious of heart,
deep in knowledge,
free from formalities.

The Companions of the Prophet were truly the blossoms of Islam's spring season and best products of the Prophet's miraculous disciplining power.

Bases of Character Building

When the Prophet, blessings and peace be on him, departed from the world and, thus, the opportunity of benefitting directly from his company came to an end, the Holy Quran, the illustrious Traditions and biography of the Prophet remained the only sources for Muslims to fill the gap. The laws and wise methods dealing with the internal part of man's self which were developed on the basis of these sources served as permanent and universal guidelines to treat sickness of the heart, insurgence of the ego, and intrigues of the devil.

The material found in the books of Hadith falls into two categories. The first category comprises Traditions dealing with the external form of deeds, such as standing, bowing, sitting and prostrating in the prayer, recitation of the Quran, remembrance of Allah, supplication, missionary endeavour, holy war, and treating friends and foes in war and peace. The second category is related to the internal state of heart and mind, such as sincerity and trust in Allah, patience and humbleness, piety and God-consciousness, generosity and kindness. These fine qualities, which are the true essence of good deeds, may never be fully appreciated by people unless there is an exemplary figure in front of them. And, undoubtedly, the best and most reliable model in whom we find these qualities in the richest and sinceremost form is the plain and simple life of the Prophet of Islam.

Noble Qualities of the Prophet:
a Comprehensive Description

We will present in this section testimonies about the moral excellence and superbness of the Prophet of Allah by two of his Companions, Hind bin Abi Hala (son of *Ummul M'umineen* Khadija and maternal uncle of Hasan and Hussain) and Ali ibn Abi Talib--may Allah be pleased with all of them. These two Companions observed the Prophet in the private and the public, knew very closely the individual, family, and social aspects of his life, and had a reputation for relating their observations authentically. Hind bin Abi Hala says:

"The Prophet of Allah, blessings and peace be on him, was always deeply engrossed in concern for life-after-death and in thoughts relating to matters of the hereafter. This mood continued to prevail on him in such a way that he could not get rest at any time. He often kept long silence and did not speak unless there was a need. When he talked, he spoke clearly until he finished. His talk was clear and straightforward; it was neither unnecessarily long nor unnecessarily short. He was mild in temper and soft in tongue, not rude or inconsiderate. He did not insult anybody nor did he like anybody to insult him. He deeply appreciated a gift of Allah, always considered it great even if it was small (to the extent that it might not easily be seen), and never found fault with it. He neither showed dislike for a food item nor indulged in admiring it. If anything unpleasant happened to him relating to things of the world, he never got angry, but if a right of Allah was violated, nothing could withstand his wrath until he took revenge. When he moved his hand [during a conversation] to express himself, he moved it fully. When he expressed surprise, he turned his hand upside down. During a talk, he used to touch the palm of his right hand with the thumb of his left hand. If a thing displeased him, he turned his face against it, ignored it, and kept quiet. When he was happy, he lowered his gaze. His laughing was often a smile in which his teeth, which were as bright and clean as hailstones, became visible."

And Ali ibn Abi Talib, another prominent Companion and close associate of the Prophet, describes his qualities in the following words:

"By nature he was averse to aspersion, lewdness and indecency and never indulged in any such act even under pressure of a situation. He did not ever talk loudly in the market. He did not return evil with evil; instead, he preferred to forgive. He never raised his hand on anybody, except in a Holy War. He never hit a slave or a woman. I did not see him taking revenge form anybody for a personal offence, except when a person violated the limits established by Allah. If a commandment of Allah the Almighty was violated and put to disgrace, he became extremely angry at the offender. When he had a choice between two things, he always preferred the convenient one. When he came to his house, he lived like an ordinary person: he himself washed his clothes, milked his goats, and performed other household chores.

"He guarded his tongue and spoke only about things which concerned him. He was courteous with people and did not make them unhappy. If a respectable person of a tribe or community visited him, he showed respect to him and appointed him to a respectable post. He was careful in making comments about others and did not deprive them of pleasant and courteous treatment on his part. He remained informed about his Companions and inquired of their conditions from others.

"He highlighted the good aspect of a virtue and thus strengthened it and exposed the bad aspect of an evil and thus weakened it. His ways were moderate and consistent. He did not remain careless toward a thing lest others should also become careless toward it and lose interest in it. He was prepared for all situations. He neither lagged behind in attending to the just rights of others, nor overacted in this regard. The persons staying close to him were the best and the selected ones. The best person in his sight was he whose sympathies and courtesies reached people in general. He held him highest in esteem who was most sympathetic, most compassionate, most helpful.

"He stood from his seat with remembrance of Allah on his tongue and sat with remembrance of Allah on his tongue. When he came upon a gathering, he took a seat at the end of it and also instructed others to do the same. He gave full attention to each person attending his company. Each person present in his gathering thought that he was closest to him. If a person asked him to sit with him for some purpose or talked with him about a personal need, he listened to him with due attention and patience until he finished and departed. If a person asked him for help, he did not let him return without fulfilling his needs; at the least he talked to him in reply in a soft and courteous way. His courtesy was open for all and he had assumed a fatherly character for them.

"Everybody was equal in his sight in matters of justice. His gathering was a seat of knowledge and cognizance, modesty and bashfulness, patience and trust. In it neither voices were raised, nor blemishes mentioned, nor honour and prestige challenged, nor weaknesses publicized. All enjoyed equal status; the superiority of one to others was only on the basis of piety (*Taqwa*). His Companions treated elders with respect and youngers with kindness and affection. They preferred the needy to themselves, protected travellers and newcomers and took care of them."

Ali, may Allah be pleased with him, further says:

"The Prophet, blessings and peace be on him, had a pleasant countenance and looked cheerful all the time. He was mild in manners and nature.[1] He was not rude by nature, nor was he used to speak impolitely or shout at others. He did not indulge in cheap talk, nor aspersed others. He was not miser. If he did not like something, he ignored it (i.e. did not accuse a person for it); but he did not clearly reject it nor did he answer questions about it. He had saved himself fully from three things: quarreling, pride, and getting involved in unnecessary affairs. He had also protected others from three things: he did not speak ill of others, nor cast aspersions on them, nor became

---

[1]That is to stay, he was quick in showing kindness and love and easily forgave people. Some scholars interpret this statement to mean that he did not enter into disputes and controversies. One scholar holds that it refers to the qualities of poise, respectability, and fear of Allah characterizing the Prophet's personality.

talked, the persons attending his gathering used to lower their heads in respect (to listen to him attentively in a motionless posture) as if birds were sitting on their heads. When he stopped talking, only then they conversed among themselves. They never entered into an argument with one another in his presence. When a person talked in his gathering, all others carefully listened until he finished. Everybody had an equal opportunity to speak in front of him (i.e. he could express himself to his satisfaction and others listened to him with due care and attention). If people laughed at a thing, he also laughed at it; if they expressed surprise at a thing, he also expressed surprise at it. He showed patience and forbearance in face of the indiscipline o travellers visiting him and in listening to their varied questions until his Companions drew the attention of such people toward themselves (and thus changed the topic). He did not talk while someone else was talking and never interrupted the talk of anyone. But if a person started crossing the limits of propriety in his talk, he either asked him to stop or left the gathering, thus obliging him to discontinue.

"He was the most generous, open-hearted, truthful, mild and kind in social matters and mutual dealings. When a person saw him for the first time, he was awed, but after living in his company for some time and knowing him closely, he began to adore him wholeheartedly. The person describing him says that he saw none like him before or after, may Allah's blessings and peace descend on him."[2]

---

[2]From *Shemaeli Tirmidhi,* quoted from *Nabie Rahmat* (Urdu) by the author (Lucknow: Academy of Islamic Research and Publications, 1978).

Moral Excellence of the Prophet

Anas bin Malik reports about the moral qualities of the Prophet in these words:

"The Prophet, blessings and peace be on him, was the most open-hearted, mild-natured, and of the noblest descent. He did not keep himself aloof from his Companions: he mixed with them closely, talked to them, and greeted their children pleasantly. He lifted their children in arms, accepted invitation from everybody--slave or free, a maidservant, or any other poor or indigent person--visited the sick even if they lived at the outskirts of the city, and accepted apology."

He was not seen stretching his legs in the gathering of his Companions so as not to cause inconvenience to anybody. His Companions recited poetic verses to one another and listened to such recitations from one another. Sometimes when they talked about matters and events of the past days of ignorance, he remained quiet or smiled. He was extremely kind, loving, and affectionate. He used to tell his daughter Fatima, may Allah be pleased with her, "Call my both sons (i.e. his grandsons Hasan and Hussain)". When they came running to him, he kissed them and hugged them close to his heart (*Timidhi*). One of his grandsons was laid in his lap in the condition that he was about to breathe his last. Tears started streaming down his eyes. S'ad, may Allah be pleased with him, inquired [about his tears], "O Prophet of Allah! What is it?" The Prophet replied, "This is mercy which Allah puts in the hearts of the bondsmen for whom He wishes so. And, indeed, Allah shows mercy to those of His bondsmen who are merciful to others" (*Bukhari*).

When the Prophet, blessings and peace be upon him, heard the groans of Abbas, his uncle who was tied with rope with other captives of the Battle of Badr, he could not sleep all night out of restlessness. On learning about it, his Companions from Madinah untied Abbas. They also expressed willingness to set him free without ransom, but the Prophet did not agree to it.

He was benign and benevolent and was very careful and considerate in dealing with people. He always took into consideration man's natural weakness of at times becoming dull, unenthusiastic and unaspiring. That is why, he delivered sermons with a gap of time so that people did not get tired. If he heard a baby crying, he shortened congregational prayers and said, "I stand to perform prayers and wish to offer them long, but when I hear the cries of a baby I cut the prayers short so that the baby's mother (praying in congregation) may not suffer."

He used to say, "Do not speak against each other to me because I wish to meet you in the condition that my heart is clean". He was kind to Muslims like a father. He used to say, "If a person leaves behind a property after his death, it belongs to his descendants. But if he leaves behind a loan he owes to somebody, it is my responsibility to pay it off". He was free from all excesses and exaggerations. Aisha, may Allah be pleased with her, bears witness that whenever the Prophet had a freedom to choose between two things, he always chose the one which was easier, provided there was no fear of any transgression in it. If there was any doubt that an act might be sinful, he stayed far away from it. He used to say that Allah liked to see that His bondsmen exhibited signs of His favours on them.

He lived at home like an ordinary person. Aisha, may Allah be pleased with her, said, "He used to wash his clothes, milk his goats, and do other household chores. He used to stitch patches in his dress and mend his shoes." When once it was inquired of Aisha how the Prophet lived at home, she replied, "He took care of household affairs. When the time of prayer arrived, he went out." She added, "He was the most kind and considerate person and always has a smiling countenance". Anas, may Allah be pleased with him, said, "I did not know a person who was more kind to his family members than the Prophet of Allah, blessings and peace be on him." Aisha, may Allah be pleased with her, reports the Prophet of Allah as saying, "The best among you is he who is the best for his family, and I am the best for my family". Abu Huraira, may Allah be pleased with him, says that the Prophet of Allah, blessings and peace be upon him, never found fault with a food item. If he liked it, he ate; if he did not like, he left it". Anas, may Allah be pleased with him, says, "I served the Prophet of Allah for ten years, but he never said to me a word expressing his displeasure, nor did he ever scold me for doing a thing or for not doing it". His Companions did not rise at his arrival to show respect to him as he did not like it. He used to tell them, "Do not exaggerate in praising me as the Christians did with Isa ibn Maryam (Jesus, son of Mary). I am simply a bondsman of Allah; so call me Allah's bondsman and prophet." Anas, may Allah be pleased with him, says, "Any maidservant or slave woman of Madinah felt free to hold the Prophet by his hand and tell him whatever she had to say and ask him to accompany her as far as she needed."

When Adi bin Hatim visited the Prophet, he was called in. The maidservant brought a pillow for the Prophet to rest upon. He put it between Adi and himself and took a seat on the floor. Adi said that from this gesture he became sure that the Prophet did not see himself as a king. Once when a person saw him, he trembled in awe. Upon this the Prophet told him, "Do not be afraid. I am not a king. I am son of a woman from the Quraish tribe who used to eat dried meat". He used to clean his house, tie the camels, feed them, eat even with the maidservant in the family, help her in kneading the flour, and buy things of daily use for the family from the market.

If he came to know about something unpleasant against a person, he did not denounce him by specifically identifying him. He rather said indirectly, "What has happened to people that they do or say such a thing". Thus he used to discourage a person from doing a bad thing without mentioning his name.

He was merciful to animals and instructed people to treat them with kindness. He said, "Allah has commanded to treat everything properly and kindly. Thus, if you have to behead a person, do it in a proper way. If you have to sacrifice an animal, do it in a proper way. He who wants to slaughter an animal should first sharpen his knife well and keep his animal comfortable". He also said, "Fear Allah in regard to animals which cannot speak. If you ride on them, do it in a proper way. If you slaughter them for meat, do it in a way that they are made comfortable as much as possible".

He also used to instruct people to treat their servants, attendants and slaves in the best possible human way and said, "Feed them what you yourselves eat. Dress them as you dress yourselves. Do not torture the creatures of Allah. Those whom Allah has made your subordinates are your brothers, attendants and helpers. Thus, if a person's brothers are his subordinates, he should feed them what he eats and dress them as he dresses himself. Do not ask them to do a job which is beyond their powers. If it can not be avoided, help them by sharing their work. "Once a Bedouin came to him and asked how many times he should forgive his servant. He replied, "Seventy times". He then added, "Pay off a labourer before his sweat dries up."[3]

Noble Manners of the Prophet

It is human nature that man tries to emulate even such qualities and behaviours of his ideal in religion which are not legally binding on him to qualify for the faith. Out of true love and admiration he makes every effort to learn not only about his ideal's prominent qualities, habits, likes and dislikes, but also about minor details relating to his manners, disposition, dress and such other things. This is the reason which has led the Muslim scholars from the past to this day to write exhaustive and detailed descriptions of the Prophet's personality, as Muslims trust, adore and emulate the Prophet with utmost sincerity. The most popular among such books is the biographical work by Imam Tirmidhi. A brief extract from this work describing the Prophet's qualities is given below.

[3]The extracts in this section are from author's book *Nabi-e-Rahmat*, Vol. II (Lucknow: Academy of Islamic Research and Publications, 1978), pp. 174-209. References are documented in the original book.

"When the Prophet of Allah, blessings and peace be on him, walked, it looked as if he was descending down to a lower plain. When he became attentive to a person, he turned his whole body toward him. He kept his gaze low; he looked at the ground more than he looked at the sky. He looked generally from the side of his eyes. While walking, he put his Companions ahead and himself remained behind them. He was first to say *Salam* (to greet) to whomever he met.

"His hair covered half of his ears: it was longer than the locks which are only upto the upper tips of the ears and shorter than the locks which fall on the shoulders. His hair was, thus, neither very long nor very short; it was of moderate size. .

"He sometimes parted his hair in such a way that a line through the hair was created. He used to oil his hair very often and combed his beard frequently. When he began to make *Wudu* (ablution), or comb, or wear shoes, he preferred to start from the right. He had a kohl case from which he used to anoint his eyes three times each. He liked *Kurta* (long shirt) most among his clothes. When he put on a new dress, he mentioned its name (to express his happiness). For example, he said that Allah blessed him with a *Kurta* (long shirt) or turban or sheet. Then he recited the following supplication:

O Allah! You alone
deserve all praise
and to You I
extend thanks for
providing this dress.
O Allah! from You

alone I seek the
good of this dress
and fulfillment of
the virtuous purposes
for which it was
made. And I seek
refuge in You from
its evil and the
evil purposes for which
it was made.

"He used to say, 'Wear white dress. One should wear white while alive and should be clothed in white when put to grave. White is one of the best colours to wear'. Once Najjashi, the ruler of Ethiopia, sent him a pair of plain black socks. He put it on and also did *Masah* on it after performing *Wudu* (ablution). He also offered prayers in such shoes which had patches of another kind of leather. He said that nobody should walk with only one shoe on; he should either wear both shoes or put both shoes off. He forbade people from eating with the left hand or wearing only one shoe. He used to say that people should put on shoes with the right foot first and put them off with the left foot first. He sometimes wore a ring in his right hand. He also got a ring made for him which had three lines carved in it: *Muhammad* in the first line, *Rasul* in the second, and *Allah* in the third. When he went to the lavatory, he took the ring off.

"When he entered Makkah on the occasion of its conquest, he had a black turban on him. When he used to put on a turban, he let one end of it fall behind in the middle of his shoulders. Ubaid bin Khalid al-Maharbi, may Allah be pleased with him, reports that once when he was walking in a street in Madinah al-Munawwara, he heard someone telling him from behind to raise his *lungi* (a dress worn in place of trousers) above his ankles (as it was lowered down over his ankles in the fashion of the rich). When he turned to the person he saw that it was the Prophet of Allah, blessings and peace be on him. He submitted to the Prophet that it was only an ordinary piece of cloth (and could not be taken as a mark of pride characterizing the arrogant rich). The Prophet said, "Do you not have my ways for you to follow." When he looked at the *lungi* of the Prophet, it was half way up to his shins.

"He did not eat in a reclining position and said, "I do not eat while reclining". After finishing his meals he licked his fingers three times. He did not eat in such a way that the food was put on a table (while he himself sat on the floor), nor did he eat in small dishes (characterizing lavish and luxurious lifestyle), nor was thin bread ever cooked for him. Once it was inquired of Qatada, may Allah be pleased with him, as to on what the Prophet put his meal while eating. He replied that food was put on a piece of (processed) leather specified for this purpose. He liked bottle-gourd (*Kaddu*) and also sweets and honey. He liked the meat of the goat's front leg. Aisha, may Allah be pleased with her, explains that, in fact, meat was rarely available to him and that he liked the meat of goat's front leg only because it took less time in tendering. This way he was able to finish eating quickly and then devoted himself to his virtuous engagements. He also liked the food left over in the cooking pot and bowl.

"He used to say, 'If a person eats without glorifying Allah, the Devil joins him'. He also said, 'If a person forgets to say *Bismillah* ("with the name of Allah") before he starts eating, he should say these words:

With the name
of Allah in the
beginning and
at the end.

He used to say the following supplication after finishing his meal:

All praise is
for Allah Who
gave us food
and drink and
raised us among
Muslims.

After he had finished eating and the remaining food was removed, he used to say the following words:

Profuse, worthy, and
abundant praise
be to Allah of
Whom we cannot
be independent, nor
can we forsake Him.
He is our Cherisher.

He used to say, 'Allah is pleased with a person who glorifies Him when he eats or drinks.'

"His favourite drink was cool and sweet water. He said, 'There is nothing like milk for food or drink'. He drank the *Zamzam* water standing. He used to drink water in three breaths.

"He had a perfume box from which he took out perfume to apply. (If anybody offered perfume as gift), he did not decline to accept. He used to say, 'Three things should not be turned down: pillow, perfume and milk'. He said that the perfume used by men should be strong in scent but unnoticeable in colour, whereas the perfume for women should be dominant in colour but mild in scent.

"Aisha, may Allah be pleased with her, said, 'The Prophet of Allah, blessings and peace be on him, did not talk hastily like you people'. His talk was clear and each point he made was so clearly distinguishable from other points that the listeners had no difficulty in understanding it. (Sometimes) he repeated his statement (out of need) three times so that his listeners could clearly understand him. He smiled instead of laughing aloud. Abdullah bin Harith says that he did not see anybody more smiling than the Prophet of Allah. Sometimes he laughed in such a way that his (front) teeth were visible. Jareer bin Abdullah says that the Prophet of Allah never stopped him from visiting him since his acceptance of Islam and he smiled when he saw him. Anas, may Allah be pleased with him, says, 'The Prophet of Allah frankly mixed with us and spoke with us in a witty and amusing way. I had a brother.

The Prophet used to ask him, 'O Abu Umair, where did the chick go?⁴ Once his Companions submitted to him, 'You sometimes talk amusingly to us'. He replied, 'Yes, but I never say anything wrong.' He sometimes recited a couplet of Abdullah bin Rawaha, a famous Arab poet, or of some other poet to make a point. He sometimes recited the following line composed by Turfa:

> *"Sometimes he brings news to*
> *you to whom you did not pay*
> *any remuneration."*

He used to say that of all poetic sayings the truest is the following statement of Labid bin Rabi'a:

> *"Know that all things in*
> *this world are mortal*
> *except Allah."*

Once one of his fingers was hit with a stone and started bleeding. On it he recited the following couplet:

> *"You are merely a finger which*
> *did not receive any injury*
> *except that you bled. (This,*
> *too, did not go in vain because)*
> *this injury was met in*
> *Allah's way."*

---

⁴Abu Umair, a young boy, had a chick which he kept in a cage and with which he used to play. It died. The Prophet used to ask him amusingly about it this way.

And in the Battle of Hunain he was reciting the following couplet:

"Indeed I am a Prophet
and I am from the progeny
of Abdul Muttalib. "

The Prophet, blessings and peace be on him, also permitted others to recite verses and even gave a prize on a poetic composition as a token of appreciation.[5] Jabir bin Samura, may Allah be pleased with him, relates that he attended more than a hundred gatherings of the Prophet, blessings and peace be on him, in which his Companions recited verses and related stories and events of the days of Ignorance and he (did not stop them and) listened to them quietly and even sometimes smiled with them. He ordered a pulpit to be put in the mosque for Hassan bin Thabit so that he could recite verses in his support from there (against the unjust criticism of the unbelievers). He also said that Allah helped Hassan through *Ruhul Quds* (the Archangel Jibrail) until he defended Islam or the Prophet through his poetic compositions.

When he prepared to rest, he put his right hand under his right check and said:

Lord! when You
raise Your bondsmen,
grant me protection
from Your punishment.

---

[5]The Prophet, blessings and peace be on him, listened to a poem by Ka'ab bin Malik and awarded him a sheet.

143

When he went to bed, he said:

O Allah! with Your
name I die and
(with it) I come to life.

When he woke up, he prayed:

All praise is for
Allah Who brought us
to life after having put
us to death and we
have to return to
Him.

The bed in which he rested was made of leather and was filled with the bark of date tree. He visited the sick and attended the burial. He accepted the invitation even of slaves. When he performed pilgrimage, he rode a camel which had an old *Hawdah* on it covered with an ordinary piece of cloth not worth even four dirhams (a meagre amount). He used to say that if a gift as humble as a goat's leg was offered to him he would accept it, and that if he was invited by somebody he would surely go to his house. One of his noble manners was that if he did not like a thing he did not tell so directly to the person concerned. He accepted gifts and gave gifts in return. In modesty he excelled even a maiden (guarding herself in cover). Whenever there was something unpleasant, its effect was immediately reflected in his face.

Position of Mankind in Islam: Man Vicegerent of Allah

Man, according to the teachings of Islam, is the representative and vicegerent of Allah on earth. This world is a trust and man is its trustee. It is not a personal property of an individual or people which could be used or misused to satisfy personal desires. It is man's responsibility to manage the world according to Allah's instructions and promote divine guidance. This great world--including animals, birds, trees, rivers, mountains, gold, silver, and all it contains--has been given to the care of man because he is more familiar than any one else with the world (as he is himself made of dust) and has also a genuine interest in it. Thus, because he has knowledge of the world and interest in it--two essential conditions for a successful trustee--he can be a good caretaker of the world.[6]

Man Most Suitable for Managing the World

When Allah created Adam and made him His vicegerent on earth, the angels who are innocent and do not commit sins, submitted to Allah that as man was inclined to quarrel and shed blood on earth, the vicegerency might be granted to them as they glorified Him and remained engaged in worshipping

[6]In view of the sad and serious persecution of human beings in different forms today the author (Sayyid Abul Hasan Ali Nadwi) started an all India movement called "The Message of Humanity" (*Payame Insaniyat*). It has held meetings, seminars, and public gatherings all over India, developed and distributed literature in different Indian languages emphasizing sublime responsibilities of man, and tried to provide a platform for people from all religions who share this common concern. For more information contact: Office of the Message of Humanity, P.O. Box 93, Lucknow, India.

Him all the time. Allah replied the angels that they did not know the matters of the world. He then tested Adam and the angels by asking them certain questions relating to the world. As Adam was made of dust and had a natural interest in the world, he answered Allah's questions correctly whereas the angels lacking this natural interest in the things of the world failed. Thus Allah established that in spite of all weaknesses man alone was most suitable for managing the world. In fact, his natural weaknesses themselves qualified him for this position. If the world were run by angels, most gifts of God put into it, which were discovered and developed by man due to his interest and need, would have remained unknown and unused.

Successful Vicegerent

But we have to remind ourselves that a vicegerent and representative has a duty to fully follow the instructions of his master. His personality and precept should reflect the values of his master. To act as a vicegerent of Allah on earth requires that man must inculcate in himself His qualities which should mould his manners. We have been taught that the qualities and attributes of Allah include knowledge, mercy, appreciativeness, administrative ability, forgiveness, benevolence, justice, love, grandeur, beauty, and power to protect and punish. Prophet Muhammad, blessings and peace be on him, taught mankind to acquire Allah's attributes ("Adorn yourself with the qualities of Allah").

In spite of inherent limitations, man can, on the limited human scale, develop in himself attributes of Allah. He can never be God, but he can exhibit Allah's great attributes in his character as Allah's vicegerent. One can imagine that if man becomes mindful of his responsibility as Allah's vicegerent on earth and thus strives to inculcate in himself divine moral attributes. how high he can rise as a human being and how pleasant and prosperous the world can become under his vicegerency. Religion, as a matter of fact, provides man with the sublimest and most balanced concept of life. It grants him a position as Allah's vicegerent, responsible for administering things on earth as His representative and functioning as a caretaker of this great trust, which brings upon mankind an unprecedented honour.

Two Contradictory Ideologies

But by the passage of time human beings developed two contradictory ideologies about man's role in life: at some places man was elevated to the position of God while at others he was degraded to the status of animals. Some human beings declared themselves as gods and some others accepted for themselves a status even lower than that of animals thinking that they lived only for the fulfillment of their physical desires. Of course, both the views are wrong. Man is neither God nor animal; he is *man* and as such Allah's deputy on earth. The world is created for him and he is created for Allah. The world is responsible to him and he is responsible to Allah. He is first and last a trustee and caretaker of the world and the realization of this fact on the part of man alone can let him run the world smoothly. History bears testimony that whenever man relinquished this ideology--by trying t o take the place of God

147

and projecting himself as the master of the world, or by stooping down to be contented with the life of animals, or by shunning the responsibility of administration of the world as its trustee and thus running away from his responsibilities and duties on the earth--he soon met humiliation and brought a tremendous loss to the world, too.

Mutual Love and Cooperation

Allah reminds the Muslims that although they were divided into bitter opponent camps before Islam, He by His grace united their hearts and made them love one another like brothers. The verse in the Quran bearing this reminder has a reference to a real situation in the Prophet's time.

When the Prophet of Allah, blessings and peace be on him, proclaimed the message of Islam in Makkah, the people there opposed him and his mission so severely that worshipping Allah in Makkah became difficult. The Makkans did not realize due to their ignorance how sincerely the Prophet wished them well. He wished to take them out of the depth of ignorance and raise them as a nation which would spread light of love through a faith all over the world. He wished to promote love in the world so that disputes and differences throughout the world might come to an end forever. He wanted to establish that man was created for a purpose and that in the absence of man's realization of that purpose his best faculties were grossly misused. One nation was fighting with another nation, one country was opposing another country, one community was inimical to another community. Mutual trust

148

and love had ceased to inspire human relationships and disobedience to Allah was common. Man hunted man as mercilessly as he hunted animals in the forest.

When it became impossible for the Prophet and his Companions to follow Islam in Makkah, they emigrated to Madinah for their faith was dearer to them than the birth-place. On arriving Madinah, they saw that the people there, specially the Aws and the Khazraj tribes, were sharply divided and had been shedding one another's blood on petty issues for long. They did so because they did not have any noble aim in front of them. When the Prophet and his Companions introduced to them the message of Islam, the members of the warring tribes of Aws and Khazraj saw the beaming promise of love and tolerance beckoning upon them. They accepted Islam, buried their long-standing hatred for ever and were united as loving brothers. Their common love for Allah and the Prophet washed away all bitterness from their hearts and they started feeling ashamed of their past.

When once the *Ansar* (residents of Madinah) and *Muhajireen* (emigrants from Makkah) accidentally picked up a quarrel at a water well, the Prophet gave his historic call to them by saying, "Kick out such a dirty thing" and reminded them of the blessings of unity and mutual love. With Islam and with the training of the Prophet the *Muhajireen* and *Ansar* as well as the warring tribes of Madinah were so much transformed that in a battlefield an injured Muslim died thirsty insisting that another wounded Muslim breathing his last next to him be given water first. The true love for Allah and the Prophet created in them such a sincere love for one another that, for example, the Muslim residents of Madinah gave equal share to the Muslim emigrants from Makkah in their shops, fields and all other kinds of property.

Malice a Serious Evil

The thing that the Prophet of Allah, blessings and peace be on him, has denounced most after *Shirk* (ascribing partners to Allah) is malice. It is related in a Tradition that in the Night of Deliverance in which Allah generously forgives the sinful, three kinds of people are not granted forgiveness: persons disobedient to their parents, habitual drunkards, and those who nourish ill-will and malice for other Muslims. The Prophet, blessings and peace be on him, has specially instructed Muslims to remain mindful of the rights of relationship on one another. It comes in another Hadith that the Prophet, blessings and peace be on him, said that Allah had ordered him to do nine things, one of which was "that I establish relationship with him who severs relationship with me, forgive him who offends me, and give him who withholds from me." It is not really a matter of credit that one should treat those courteously with whom he has good relationship. Islam urges upon its adherents that they treat even those with courtesy and goodwill who hurt them.

VI

CONCLUSION

God Not Disappointed with Man

Allah's attitude toward the human race is just opposite to man's attitude toward it. Allah is not disappointed with man. His divine blessings and favours are constantly descending upon human beings. Each new-born baby proclaims that Allah has not lost hope in mankind. Each drop of rain falling from the sky and grain of crop coming out from the earth reflects that Allah is not disappointed with man. The sun rises every morning without fail to provide light and heat to mankind; the moon shines in the sky at night with regularity and spreads its cool and soothing light over the world. Among the myriad majestic and elegant creations of Allah, man remains the most wonderful, and is the dearest to Allah. It is he for whom the whole world is created and for whom it is maintained.

But now-a-days man shows from his behaviour that the human race, the best creation of God, deserves no respect. Man hates man, exploits him, oppresses him, and kills him as if there is no good in him. It seems that man wishes to plead in the court of Allah himself that the human race deserves annihilation. It seems that man wishes to prove that the angels were right in submitting to Allah at the time of his creation that he would cause destruction on earth and shed blood.

Value of Love

But there is an exceptional glare of love in man's eyes which is not found in any other creature. His heart is characterized with a softness and melting quality inspired by love and quivers with the touch of pain and suffering for others. Such a heart is not in the treasures of the angels and surely man alone can present to his Lord a heart full of sincere love for others.

The excellence of man lies in his love and mercy for others: one person is pricked with a thorn but another person feels the pain. Man is gifted with tears which fall from his eyes when he sees a widow's head uncovered in helplessness, a poor man's kitchen unlit, and a sick man in distress. If such a drop of tear is put in a sea of transgression, it will cleanse it. If it falls on a forest of sins, it will burn it and fill the space again with the effulgence of virtue. The angels can bring forward anything, but they cannot present this drop of tear. The angels do not sleep due to their cognizance of Allah's being and attributes, but their vigil does not have the excellence of man's inability to sleep due to the sufferings of others.

The quality of love permeating through the human heart is a very precious gift of God. When something stirs it, it assumes a strange power. It rises above the considerations of religion, community, nation, and motherland. It then only sees another man's heart and feels its suffering and is drawn to it by nature as is pulled an iron chip toward a magnet.

Sharing Other's Sufferings
Man's Chief Excellence

If man loses the ability of sharing other's sufferings, he will become bankrupt. Even if a nation is blessed with the wealth of America, administration of Russia, and petrol wells of Saudi Arabia, even if rivers of gold and silver flow in it, and even if wealth showers over its land like rain, it will still be truly pauper if its stream of love is dried. The blessings of Allah will not descend on it. It is a matter of great satisfaction that man's eyes can still shed tears and that his heart can still suffer with the pain of others. The heart which loses this quality is not a heart; it is just a piece of stone. Such a heart has no value in the sight of Allah, no matter whether it is the heart of a Muslim, or a Hindu, or a Christian. The value of the human heart, in fact, lies in its quality to long, shiver, cry, and love. The human heart should be greener than the land, broader than the universe, more affluent than the waterfall, and more bountiful than the heavy clouds ready to stream down.

The eye which does not become wet is not a human eye; it is the eye of a daffodil. The heart which does not feel pain of others is not a human heart; it is the heart of a lion. The forehead which does not become wet with the perspiration of penitence is not a human forehead; it is a piece of rock. The hand which does not move forward to serve humanity is virtually paralysed and lifeless. The claw of a lion is better than that hand of a person which cuts the throat of another human being. Had the Creator wished man to live to kill, He would have created man with swords in place of hands. If the aim of man's creation were to store wealth, he would have been born with an iron safe in place of a throbbing heart. If man had been created to plan destruction, he were born with a devil's mind instead of man's.

People marvel at the wonders of man's physical self but the wonders of man's heart are so much more curious. Man has such a sensitive heart that if one person suffers in the east, another person feels the pain in the west. It was the same kind of heart which kept the Prophet of Allah restless at home all night because the non-Muslim captives of the Battle of Badr (who were his arch enemies) were tied down and groaned in pain. It was the same sympathetic human heart which made him shorten his prayers when he heard a baby crying, thinking that its mother praying behind him in congregation might become restless. How can then a heart be called a heart if it inflicts pain on another heart?

Man's Ultimate Responsibility

If human beings subjugate themselves to the supremacy of material things and become slaves to their selfish desires, life on earth will become hellish and unbearable. Man has to remember that his place in the scheme of creation is that of God's vicegerent. As the Quran bears testimony, Allah ordered the angels to bow down in front of man as a mark of respect. This clearly establishes that it is highly humiliating for man, God's deputy on earth, to bow down in front of anybody except his Creator. Had there been any such scope, Allah should have allowed man to bow down in front of the angels as they carry on Allah's orders on the earth: they, for instance, bring rain and make the wind blow. By making the angels bow down in front of man Allah clearly revealed His will that the world has been given to the care of man as His vicegerent and that he himself is created for the worship of Allah the Almighty. Man must look at his present miserable lot and tell himself that he is supposed to do better. He must rise to his appointed position as Allah's vicegerent, take none else except Allah as his Lord, and save himself and the world from eternal suffering.

www.ingramcontent.com/pod-product-compliance
Lightning Source LLC
Chambersburg PA
CBHW070729130525
26554CB00045B/752